THE
BRIDGE PLAYER'S DICTIONARY

Compiled and Edited by
Randall Baron

Published by
Devyn Press, Inc.
Louisville, Kentucky

Dedication

To Lois and C.D.
who taught me almost everything I have learned.

Printed in the United States of America.

Devyn Press, Inc.
3600 Chamberlain Lane, Suite 230
Louisville, KY 40241
1-800-274-2221

ISBN 0-939460-50-5

Acknowledgements

A large part of this book was first published in England by Mr. Bridge. We gratefully thank him for his full cooperation, along with his compiler Giles Thompson and his editors David Parry, Simon Ainger and Eric Crowhurst.

Jude Goodwin-Hanson for her unique cartoons.

Betty Mattison for her tireless typesetting.

Ralph "The Buffalo" Letizia and James Maier for their proof-reading/editing.

Sue Emery and the ACBL for their classic photos.

Tony Lipka and Richard Huggard for their gracious assistance throughout the book.

A.B.A.
The American Bridge Association, founded in 1932, to encourage duplicate bridge among Afro-American bridge players.

WE	THEY
150	
100	50
50	

ABOVE THE LINE
Phrase used in rubber bridge to identify scores entered above the horizontal line on the score sheet arising from penalties, overtricks, premiums for slams, honors etc. which do not count towards game. See BELOW THE LINE, RUBBER BRIDGE.

ABSOLUTE FORCE
Refers to a bidding situation (or bid) which your partner cannot pass. An opening two club bid (artificial and forcing) is such an instance, since you may have a hand capable of producing a game all by yourself and the opening two club call is merely the start of the auction. A jump shift response by you (if this is strong in your partnership) is also an absolute force, since it should show a guaranteed game and a possible slam.

A.B.T.A.
The American Bridge Teachers Association, founded in 1957, is a professional organization of bridge teachers, directors and writers.

ACCORDING TO HOYLE
Correct legally, ethically and according to custom.

A.C.B.L.

The American Contract Bridge League. It is the national authority and sponsoring organization for most of the bridge activity in North America. The ACBL is responsible for conducting tournaments, regulating rule changes, recording member masterpoints, publishing the monthly "Bulletin" and conducting teaching programs.

ACE

The highest-ranking card in each suit.

ACE ASKING BIDS

The bid of four notrump (Blackwood) or four clubs (Gerber) are artificial bids asking the number of aces in partner's hand. These are currently the most popular ace asking bids.

ACE FROM ACE-KING

Partnerships need to agree which card is to be led from suits headed by A K. The lead of the Ace from this combination is much more common currently than in past years.

ACE LEAD

If a partnership's standard lead from A K against no trumps is the King, then the lead of the Ace is often conventionally a request for partner to play an honor if he has one, or otherwise give a count signal. If the partnership's agreed lead is Ace from A K, then the King lead can be used to ask for an unblock or count in a similar fashion.

ACE SHOWING RESPONSES

A system of responses to forcing opening bids based on the assumption that opener is more interested in partner's first round controls than in general strength. It is most commonly played in conjunction with a conventional two club opening bid. The responses are:

2♦	Negative (no Ace) and 5 or less points.
2♥, 2♠, 3♣ or 3♦	Showing the Ace of the bid suit.
2NT	Positive but Aceless.
3NT	Showing two Aces.
4NT	Showing three Aces.

See CAB.

ACES SCIENTIFIC SYSTEM

Developed by the Dallas Aces (later called The Aces) featuring a strong notrump, weak twos, 5 card majors, and 2-over-1 game forcing style.

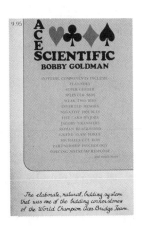

9.95

ACE ♥ ♣ ♦ ♠
SCIENTIFIC
BOBBY GOLDMAN

SYSTEMIC COMPONENTS INCLUDE:
FLANNERY
SUPER GERBER
SPLINTER BIDS
WEAK TWO BIDS
INVERTED MINORS
NEGATIVE DOUBLES
FIVE CARD MAJORS
JACOBY TRANSFERS
ROMAN BLACKWOOD
GRAND SLAM FORCE
MICHAELS CUE BIDS
PARTNERSHIP PSYCHOLOGY
FORCING NOTRUMP RESPONSE
and much more

The elaborate, natural, bidding system that was one of the bidding cornerstones of the World Champion Aces Bridge Team.

ACOL

A bidding system developed in the mid 1930s by Jack Marx and S.J.Simon. It takes its name from the Acol Bridge Club in Hampstead where the two played and began to develop their theories. They were joined by Maurice Harrison-Gray and Iain Macleod and the then relatively unknown team enjoyed immediate tournament success, thereby popularizing the system. It has remained the most widespread system in use in Britain. Since ACOL is based on natural bidding, it is widely used as a basic system for teaching bridge.

ACOL TWO-BIDS
In the Acol System, opening two-bids in all four suits are strong and forcing. Those in diamonds, hearts, and spades are usually made on unbalanced hands of less than game going strength. The two club opening may be based either on a balanced hand or on an unbalanced game-going hand.

ACTIVE DEFENSE
The defenders' approach when they are desperate for tricks because declarer threatens to obtain discards for his losers. The opposite of passive defense.

ADJUSTED SCORE
A score assigned by the Director. If the Director judges that a pair or a team has suffered because of a transgression of the laws or ethics by opponents (even though the transgression is inadvertent) he is empowered to adjust the actual score recorded to establish an equitable result.

ADVANCE CUE BID
A cue bid made when there is no apparent suit agreement. For example, in the auction 1NT - Pass - 3♠ - Pass - 4♦, the 4♦ bid is an advance cue bid. Opener's normal rebid would be either 3NT or 4♠, but here he is making a cue bid to imply that he has a good spade fit, maximum values for his 1NT opening and that he holds the A♦. He is implicitly denying the A♣ by his failure to bid 4♣. With this information available, further action is up to his partner. See CUE BID.

ADVANCE SACRIFICE (ADVANCE SAVE)
A sacrifice bid made before the opponents have reached their presumed contract.

ADVERSARY
Either LHO (left hand opponent) or RHO (right hand opponent) may be considered your adversary or foe. MHO (middle hand opponent) is a humorous term for partner who in theory is your friend.

AGGREGATE SCORE
Sum of all the scores obtained without conversion to I.M.Ps.

ALCATRAZ COUP
An illegal play which, as the name suggests, should attract a severe penalty. The following is an example:

♠ A J 9

♠ K 10 2

South, declarer, has to make three tricks in spades. Calling for the Jack from dummy and receiving a small card from his right-hand opponent he fails to follow suit. Fourth hand then either follows with the Queen or plays low. If low, declarer quickly corrects his revoke by substituting the 10. If the Queen is played declarer corrects his revoke by producing the King. His left-hand opponent can now change his card but South takes the marked finesse on the next round. See COFFEE-HOUSING.

ALERT
Sponsoring organizations often require that a conventional bid be "alerted" so that opponents become aware that it is not natural. Various ways of alerting may be specified but a common one is for the partner of the player making the conventional bid to tap on the table (in Britain) or say "alert" (in the U.S.). See CONVENTION.

ALPHA SUPPORT ASKING BIDS
In the Super Precision System of bidding, a number of different types of asking bids are used. Using Alpha Support Asking Bids, if the opener bids a new suit after a positive response to his one club opening, he is asking the responder about his overall strength (controls) and his support for the opener's suit.

AMBULANCE SERVICE
To rescue partner from a huge penalty.

ANALYSIS
The study of a hand to find the best possible line of play by declarer or defense.

ANCHOR SUIT
When some form of two-suited hand is shown, one of which is specified, the specified suit is called an anchor suit. See ASTRO.

APPEAL
A request for a review of a Tournament Director's ruling. At important events there is a procedure for requesting such a review by an Appeals Committee.

APPENDIX TABLE(S)
A useful adaptation of a Howell Movement (or occasionally a Mitchell Movement) in order to accommodate extra tables without adding to the number of boards in play.

APPROACH FORCING
The basic principle behind most modern bidding systems, whereby a change of suit is treated as forcing for one round.

ARNO
Another name for the Little Roman Club System.

ARRANGEMENT OF TRICKS
At rubber bridge one member of each partnership collects the cards played to each trick and arranges the tricks in front of him. At duplicate bridge each player retains his cards arranging them in front of him, vertically if his side won the trick and horizontally otherwise.

ARRANGING
A statement made by a player still sorting his cards to explain why he is not forthcoming with a bid.

ARTIFICIAL (CALL)
A call which carries an unnatural meaning. For example, a Stayman 2♣ says nothing about clubs, but instead inquires about partner's major suits.

ASKING BID
An asking bid is a bid made by the member of a partnership wishing to take control of the auction which requests partner to give information about his hand, but does not itself directly convey any. Blackwood is the most commonly used asking bid.

ASPRO
A variation of ASTRO devised by Terence Reese (the name is borrowed from a popular British brand of aspirin). After an opponent opens 1NT, 2♣ shows hearts and another suit and 2♦ shows spades and a minor suit. See DEFENSE TO 1NT.

ASSUMPTION
Technique by which declarer or defender bases his play on the premise that the contract can be made or set.

ASTRO

This is a conventional defense to a 1NT opening whereby minor suit overcalls show two suits with at least nine cards between them. It derives its name from its inventors, **A**llinger, **ST**ern and **RO**sler. 2♣ shows hearts and a minor and 2♦ shows spades and another suit. The major suit specified is called the anchor suit. See DEFENSE TO 1 NT.

ASTRO CUE-BID

Astro Cue-bids are used to describe two-suited hands that include one major suit and one minor suit. The cue-bid shows the lower unbid major suit and the lower unbid minor suit. Specific cue-bids show the following two suits:

> 1♣ - 2♣　shows hearts and diamonds
> 1♦ - 2♦　shows hearts and clubs
> 1♥ - 2♥　shows spades and clubs
> 1♠ - 2♠　shows hearts and clubs

See ANCHOR SUIT.

ATTACKING LEAD

A lead which positively attempts to establish tricks for the defense, as opposed to a passive lead which is simply intended to give no advantage to declarer. See PASSIVE LEAD.

Attitude Signals

ATTITUDE SIGNALS

Signals made by a defender to encourage a continuation of the suit led, or to suggest a switch. Traditionally, this is done by playing a high card to encourage and a low card to discourage.

AUCTION

Bidding by the four players for the contract; the complete bidding sequence.

AUCTION BRIDGE

The predecessor of modern Contract Bridge, Auction Bridge was first played in 1903 and the first code governing its play set up in 1908 by a joint committee of The Bath Club and The Portland Club in Britain. It gained rapid support and became more popular than similar games of the time (Bridge Whist, for example), but was quickly superseded in 1926 by Contract Bridge.

AUTOBRIDGE

A commercial device, developed in America and now manufactured in France, with which pre-dealt hands can be used for self-teaching bidding and play.

AUTOMATIC SQUEEZE

A squeeze which works automatically against either opponent. For instance:

Dummy
♠ A K Q 2
♥ 2

Your Hand
♠ 4 3
♥ K
♦ A

When you lead the ace of diamonds from your hand and discard the two of hearts from dummy, either opponent holding four spades and the heart ace will be squeezed out of protecting one of those suits.

AVERAGE (SCORE)

Half the maximum number of matchpoints available on a hand at duplicate pairs. When through its own fault a pair is unable to play a board, the tournament director will usually award an average minus (40% of the total matchpoints available) and an average plus (60% of the total) to an innocent pair unable to play a board.

AVOIDANCE PLAY

A play designed to prevent a particular opponent from gaining the lead. For example:

A K 3 2

Q 8 7   J 10 9

6 5 4

If South, declarer, wishes to take three tricks in the suit without allowing East to gain the lead, he must start by leading a small card from hand. West plays low and dummy's King wins. South now re-enters his hand and leads a second card. Again West plays low and dummy's Ace wins. The third round can then safely be lost to West. If at any stage West contributes the Queen, South simply allows him to hold the trick.

BABY BLACKWOOD
Some partnerships have adopted this low level Blackwood bid. It is a bid of three notrump by the opening bidder after the responder has made a strong forcing raise of the opener's suit. For example,

Opener	Responder
1♠	3♠
3 Notrump	

BACKWARD FINESSE
A normal finesse is the lead of a card towards a tenace position, with the intention of playing the lower of the top two cards if the missing card is not forthcoming. However if the missing card is known to be over the tenace the finesse may be taken "backwards." For example:

A 7 2

K J 9

Needing three tricks in the suit, South would normally play a small card from dummy towards the K J, playing East for the Queen. However, if South judges that West holds the Queen, he may play the Jack from hand. If West covers with the Queen, North's Ace wins and a small card is played towards the K 9 finessing East for the 10.

BACKWASH SQUEEZE

This rare and different type of squeeze was offered to the masses by Geza Ottlik through books and articles. In this squeeze an opponent is placed in the uncomfortable position of either underruffing declarer or relinquishing control of a side suit. A case in point:

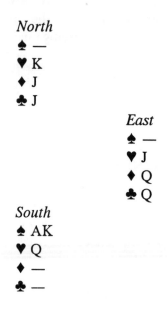

North
- ♠ —
- ♥ K
- ♦ J
- ♣ J

East
- ♠ —
- ♥ J
- ♦ Q
- ♣ Q

South
- ♠ AK
- ♥ Q
- ♦ —
- ♣ —

Hearts are trump, and declarer is locked in his hand, so if he leads a spade it will be ruffed, and if he pulls trump he will end up in the dummy and lose the last two tricks. The solution is to lead a high spade and trump it in the dummy. East must either underruff or discard his winning queen in one of the minors. If there is an underruff, declarer now trumps a minor and claims. If East discards a minor suit queen, declarer simply leads the non-established jack of that suit from dummy and East is again demolished.

BALANCE OF STRENGTH

A partnership is said to possess the balance of strength if they have more high card points than their opponents.

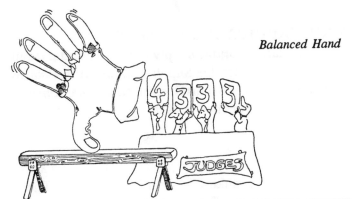

BALANCED DISTRIBUTION (OR BALANCED HAND)

Hand distributions of 4 - 3 - 3 - 3, 4 - 4 - 3 - 2 and 5 - 3 - 3 - 2 (the first of these being described as "completely balanced"). Hands of 5 - 4 - 2 - 2 or 6 - 3 - 2 - 2 distribution are sometimes described as "semi-balanced." An opening bid of 1NT usually shows a balanced hand, sometimes with the further constraint that no five card major is held.

BALANCING

When a player is in the position so that to pass would end the bidding, he is said to be in the balancing position. For instance, after the auction 1♣ - Pass - Pass, the fourth player is in the balancing position. Since partner may have a fair hand, but no suitable overcall, it is often advisable for the player in that position to bid or to double for take out, even on slender values. See TAKE OUT DOUBLE, REOPENING DOUBLE, RE-OPEN THE BIDDING.

BAROMETER SCORING

The calculation and display of results round by round rather than at the end of each session, increasing the interest for both players and spectators.

BARON (SYSTEM)

Leo Baron invented this system in the 1940s with the help of Adam Meredith. Several of their ideas have been incorporated in other systems, especially in modern Acol.

BARON BARCLAY BRIDGE SUPPLIES

The world's largest bridge supply house, located in Louisville, Kentucky. Barclay Bridge Supplies, founded in 1944 by Ruth Cohen, was originally in Port Chester, New York; it was acquired by Baron Bridge Supplies in 1990.

BARON OVER 2NT

In response to an opening bid of 2NT, a bid of 3♣ asks opener to show his lowest ranking four card or longer suit. The partners may continue to show four card suits in ascending order up to the level of 3NT.

BARON SLAM TRY

A convention whereby a bid in the suit below the agreed trump suit at the five or six level asks partner to bid a slam (small or grand) if his trump holding is better than could be expected from his previous bidding.

BARON TWO NO TRUMP RESPONSE

Stemming directly from the work of Leo Baron and his colleagues, the 2NT response to an opening suit bid at the one level is game forcing showing 16-18 points and a balanced distribution. Both opener and responder are expected to bid four card (or longer) suits upwards until a suitable fit has been located or 3NT reached.

BARRAGE

Another term for pre-emptive bidding.

BARRED

Forbidden to bid. Some infractions of the rules carry a penalty which the director will spell out for all the players. One such penalty is that a player may be barred (not allowed to participate) from bidding for one round or perhaps the entire auction.

BATH COUP
A hold-up after a King (from K Q) lead towards an Ace-Jack combination which forces the leader to switch or concede a trick to both the Ace and Jack. For example:

7 6 2

K Q 10 9 8   4 3

A J 5

West leads the King on which South plays the 5.

BATTLE OF THE CENTURY
In the winter of 1931, Culbertson challenged Sidney Lenz to a match over 150 rubbers, Lenz playing the then "official" system, and Culbertson his own. The match (dubbed "The Battle of the Century") was won by Culbertson by 8980 points and resulted in the wide acceptance of Culbertson's ideas on bidding.

BECKER CONVENTION
Used over an opponent's 1 NT opening, a bid of 2♣ shows length in both minor suits; 2♦ shows both majors.

*B. J. Becker (in the background)
with Harold Vanderbilt and
William McKenney.*

BED
A player is said to have "gone to bed with an Ace" if, having had the opportunity to cash it earlier, he fails to take it at all.

BELATED SUPPORT
See DELAYED SUPPORT.

BELONG

A hand is said to belong to a side if they can make the optimum contract.

BELOW THE LINE

Phrase used in rubber bridge to identify scores entered below the horizontal line on the score sheet. Only scores counting towards game are so entered. See ABOVE THE LINE, RUBBER BRIDGE.

BENNETT MURDER

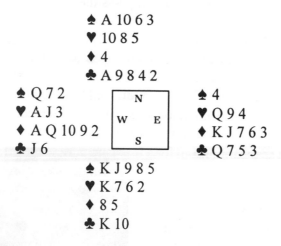

```
              ♠ A 10 6 3
              ♥ 10 8 5
              ♦ 4
              ♣ A 9 8 4 2
♠ Q 7 2                        ♠ 4
♥ A J 3          N             ♥ Q 9 4
♦ A Q 10 9 2   W   E           ♦ K J 7 6 3
♣ J 6            S             ♣ Q 7 5 3
              ♠ K J 9 8 5
              ♥ K 7 6 2
              ♦ 8 5
              ♣ K 10
```

In 1929, the Bennetts were playing the Hoffmans at the Bennetts' house in Kansas City, Missouri. South (Mr. Bennett) dealt and opened 1♠. Mr. Hoffman overcalled 2♦, and Mrs. Bennett raised to 4♠, the final contract. Mr. Hoffman led the Ace of diamonds and Mr. Bennett failed to make the contract. Throughout the evening the Bennetts had argued but, after her husband failed to make 4♠, the situation boiled over. Mrs. Bennett violently castigated Mr. Bennett, while Mr. Bennett announced his intention to "spend the night in an hotel," and subsequently "leave town." As the Hoffmans started to leave Mrs. Bennett took the family pistol from her mother's room and shot Mr. Bennett. He staggered to a chair uttering the words "She got me." On arrival, the police found Mrs. Bennett weeping over the body.

BERMUDA BOWL
See WORLD CHAMPIONSHIPS.

BETA SUIT ASKING BID
In the Super Precision System, in order to find out about the responder's holding in opener's suit after a negative response to the one club opening, the opener can jump to two hearts or two spades. The responder bids in 8 steps showing his specific holding in the suit.

BID (BIDDING)
Any call which includes the naming of a denomination and thereby undertakes to win a certain number of tricks in that denomination. Therefore double, redouble and pass are technically not bids.

BIDDABLE SUIT
A suit which complies with minimum requirements in terms of length and strength for it to be bid. A holding such as Q J x x used to be regarded as the minimum for a four card suit, while all five card suits were considered biddable. In the modern style any suit of four cards is considered biddable.

BIDDING BOXES

A Swedish invention permitting silent bidding. Each player, instead of vocally making his bid, takes a card from a complete set of indexed cards held in a small tray and places it in front of him on the table.

BIDDING SPACE

The room available for making bids. The cheaper the bid, the less bidding space used up. For example, the 1♦ bid in the auction 1♣ - Pass - 1♦ uses minimal bidding space, but 1♦ - Pass - 2♠ uses up significantly more. In constructive bidding, it is usually preferable to conserve bidding space (at least until a fit is found) in order to exchange the maximum amount of information. Conversely, it is often in the interest of the defenders to restrict the amount of space available to the opposition, for instance by making pre-emptive bids.

BIDDING SYSTEM

The sum total of partnership understandings and conventions which form the language of the bidding.

BID OUT OF TURN

The auction progresses in a clockwise manner. If a player makes a call out of this prescribed rotation (including an opening call), he has bid out of turn. Penalties may be assessed.

BIFF

Slang for trumping the suit led.

BIG CLUB

Any bidding system in which the opening bid of One Club is used for all huge opening hands (other than 2NT and 3NT). The benefits of a Big Club System are the slower approach and the methods of showing more refined information at low levels. A disadvantage of the system is that when you open 1♣ you are waving a red flag at the enemy. The opponents can jump into the auction with anything and sometimes can bid lead-directing suits at very low levels.

BIT

English slang term for a small card as in "Ace-bit" (A x).

BLACK POINTS
Master points won at club games or other competitions. They are the easiest points to acquire in the ranking system of the A.C.B.L.

BLACKWOOD (CONVENTION)
In its most basic form, a bid of 4NT when a trump suit has been agreed asks partner to show how many Aces he holds. In response:

Easley Blackwood

    5♣   Shows zero or four Aces.
    5♦   Shows one Ace.
    5♥   Shows two Aces.
    5♠   Shows three Aces.

After the response to Blackwood, 5NT may be used to ask for Kings on a similar scale. See BYZANTINE BLACKWOOD, CAB, ROLLING BLACKWOOD, ROMAN BLACKWOOD, ROMAN KEY CARD BLACKWOOD.

BLITZ
To beat a pair or team very badly. To be blitzed is to suffer this fate.

BLIZZARD
A worthless hand.

BLOCK (BLOCKED)
A suit is said to be blocked if it is impossible, without the use of an outside entry, to play out the suit by cashing top cards. For example:

A

K Q J 3

In order that the above suit may be cashed, South must possess an outside entry since the Ace will win the first trick in the North hand.

BLOCKBUSTER
A very powerful hand.

BLOCKING PLAY
A play made in an attempt to cause a block in the opponents' suit. For example:

```
                 A 2

      K J 7 6 3              Q 5

               10 9 8 4
```

West leads the 6 against South's no trump contract. The play of the Ace from dummy will block the suit. East cannot play the Queen without conceding a trick and similarly, when East is on lead and returns the Queen, West is unable to overtake without conceding a trick.

BLUE CLUB (BLUE TEAM CLUB)
System used by some of the Italian Blue Team during their long string of World Championship victories. Developed mainly by Benito Garozzo and Leon Yallouze, the system is based on an artificial 1♣ opening (17+ points) and canape. See CANAPE.

Italy's Blue Team: (left to right) Camillo Pabis Ticci, Pietro Forquet, Benito Garozzo, Massimo D'Alelio, Giorgio Belladonna and Walter Avarelli.

BLUE TEAM

The name given to the enormously successful international Italian team, so called after their triumph over the Red team in the 1956 Italian trials. From 1957 until 1975 the Blue Team won every Bermuda Bowl World Championship it contested (it did not participate in 1970/71) and the 1964, 68 and 1972 Olympiads. The three best known players in this period were Giorgio Belladonna, Pietro Forquet and Benito Garozzo. The team divided into two schools of thought over bidding, which led to the development of the Neapolitan Club (forerunner of the Blue Club) and the Roman Club. See WORLD CHAMPIONSHIPS.

BOARD

1) A device used in duplicate bridge (showing the hand number, dealer, vulnerability and compass points) with four slots to house the hands. Plastic or leather wallets are also used for the same purpose.

2) The table on which the cards are played.

3) The dummy's hand (due to its lying on the table).

BOARD-A-MATCH SCORING
(BOARD-A-MATCH TEAMS)

At teams-of-four, a form of scoring where each board is won, lost or tied. A win is 1 point, a tie 1/2 and a loss 0. The winning margin is irrelevant; +100 vs +90 or +2210 vs -1100 garners the same 1 point for the winners. See POINT A BOARD.

BODY

That part of the hand excluding the honor cards. The quality of the body can significantly influence the value of the hand, particularly in judging whether to bid marginal games.

BONUS

Different bonuses are awarded in all types of bridge.

In Rubber Bridge the bonuses are:

Vulnerable grand slam	1500
Non-vulnerable grand slam	1000
Vulnerable small slam	750
Non-vulnerable slam	500
Rubber completed in two games	700
Rubber completed in three games	500
One game in an incomplete rubber	300
Partscore in an incomplete rubber	100
Successful doubled contract	50
Successful redoubled contract	100
Five trump honors in one hand	150
Four trump honors in one hand	100
Four Aces in one hand at no trumps	150

In Chicago Bridge the bonuses are:

Vulnerable grand slam	1500
Non-vulnerable grand slam	1000
Vulnerable small slam	750
Non-vulnerable slam	500
Vulnerable game	700
Non-vulnerable game	500
Partscore on the last hand	300
Successful doubled contract	50
Successful redoubled contract	100
Five trump honors in one hand	150
Four trump honors in one hand	100
Four Aces in one hand at no trumps	150

In Duplicate Bridge the bonuses are:

Vulnerable grand slam	1500
Non-vulnerable grand slam	1000
Vulnerable small slam	750
Non-vulnerable slam	500
Vulnerable game	500
Non-vulnerable game	300
Partscore	50
Successful doubled contract	50
Successful redoubled contract	100

The Book

BOOK
The first six tricks won by the declaring side. The term originates from the practice by declarer of placing the first six tricks won in a single pile, a "book." See ODD TRICK.

BOTTOM
A score of zero matchpoints on a board in a duplicate event.

BOXED
A hand or deck of cards is said to be boxed if one or more of the cards is faced. See FACE.

BREAK
1) The distribution of the outstanding cards in a suit between the unseen hands. Also used to describe a perfectly even break (e.g. 3 - 3), or a nearly even break when an odd number of cards is missing (e.g. 3 - 2). For example: "If the clubs break ....".

2) To defeat a contract.

BRIDGE

A partnership game derived from Whist. The term is used to refer to three games: Bridge Whist, Auction Bridge and Contract Bridge. The first recorded mention of a game like Bridge was in 1886 when a pamphlet was published about the game Biritch or Russian Whist. There is little evidence to suggest that the game did originate in Russia, although it does bear a close resemblance to Vint which is a game of Russian origin. The name Bridge is simply a corruption of "Biritch." Due to the dominance of Contract Bridge, the term is nowadays considered synonymous with Contract Bridge. There are several variations of Contract Bridge including Rubber Bridge, Chicago Bridge (four deal bridge) and Duplicate Bridge (Pairs, Teams or Individuals).

BRIDGE BUFF'S BULLETIN

Newsletter for bridge book collectors. Published since 1973 by Bill Sachen of Waukegan, Illinois.

BRIDGE MAGAZINE

English magazine founded in 1926, now published in London.

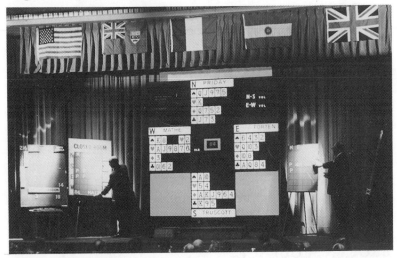

BRIDGE-O-RAMA

Method of displaying bridge to an audience. First used in the 1958 World Championship but, due to the requirement for a great number of operators, it has been replaced by Vu-Graph since the 1970s. See VU-GRAPH.

BRIDGE PLUS
English magazine based in Bisley, Surrey, published by Mr. Bridge.

BRIDGE TODAY
American magazine edited by Pam and Matt Granovetter.

BRIDGETTE
Two-handed bridge game that uses a 55 card deck (52 usual cards plus three special cards called colons). It was invented by Prince Jali Kansil and Waldemar von Zedtwitz.

BRIDGE WORLD
The oldest continuously-published magazine on contract bridge. It was founded by Ely Culbertson in 1929; the current editors are Edgar Kaplan and Jeff Rubens.

BRIDGE WORLD STANDARD
A consensus system which includes the preferences of experts, developed by Bridge World magazine.

BRING IN
To bring in a suit for three tricks means to make three tricks in that suit.

BROKEN SEQUENCE
A sequence of honor cards (but including the 9) with one of the middle cards missing, for example K J 10 9, A Q J, A K J 10.

BROKEN SUIT
Suit which contains no cards adjacent in rank.

BROZEL
Brozel allows the partnership to play in any suit at the two level over the opponent's one notrump opening. Using the Brozel convention, a double shows a one-suited hand of at least average strength. Brozel also provides a system of bids to describe two suited hands.

2♣	=	hearts and clubs
2♦	=	hearts and diamonds
2♥	=	hearts and spades
2♠	=	spades and a minor suit
2 NT	=	both minor suits

BUENOS AIRES AFFAIR
This refers to the 1965 Bermuda Bowl World Championship when the British pair, Terence Reese and Boris Schapiro, was accused of cheating by transmitting information regarding the length of their heart suits with finger signals. Although at the time the World Bridge Federation executive committee found Reese and Schapiro guilty, a subsequent independent enquiry found after ten months consideration that the charges were unfounded. Arguments for both sides may be found in the books "The Story of an Accusation" by Terence Reese and "The Great Bridge Scandal" by Alan Truscott.

BUSINESS DOUBLE
See PENALTY DOUBLE.

BUST
A seemingly useless hand.

BUSY CARD

A card which has some definite purpose in the play of a hand, as opposed to an idle card which may be safely discarded. The term usually refers to an important card in a squeeze position.

BUTCHER

Slang term meaning to misplay, especially to misplay very badly. "Carve" and "Misere" are similar terms.

BUTLER METHOD

A method of scoring duplicate pairs events in terms of I.M.Ps. The scores for each board are averaged to produce a datum score (in a large field the top and bottom scores are ignored). Each pair's score is then calculated relative to the datum and converted to I.M.P.s. See DATUM, INTERNATIONAL MATCH-POINTS (I.M.P.s).

BUY

In a competitive auction a player is said to have bought the contract if the opponents do not compete further.

BYLAWS

Rules determined by the national bridge organizations governing their membership.

BYE STAND (OR BYESTAND)

Where boards are placed when they are not in play. In a Mitchell movement, when used with a relay, a bye stand eliminates the need for a skip round.

BYZANTINE BLACKWOOD

A complex, modern version of Blackwood, based on the concept of key cards in the key suits bid by the partnership. See BLACKWOOD.

CAB
Natural system of bidding not dissimilar to Acol, particular features of which are Ace-showing responses to the 2♣ opener and Blackwood. CAB stands for two Clubs, Ace responses and Blackwood. See ACE SHOWING RESPONSES, BLACK-WOOD, TWO CLUB SYSTEMS.

CADDY
An assistant who collects scores at a tournament to help the directors.

CALCUTTA
A duplicate tournament making possible a financial gain to any player or other participant. After the entries have been made, an auction is held at which players and spectators bid to place bets on contesting pairs. The money bet is put into a pool and distributed among the purchasers of the winning pair or pairs.

CALIFORNIA CUE BID
A cue bid of the opponent's suit asking partner to bid no trump with a full or partial stopper (determined beforehand by partnership agreement) in the bid suit. Also called Western Cue Bid.

CALL
Any bid, double, redouble or pass.

CALL OUT OF ROTATION
A call made by any player when it is properly the turn of another player.

CANAPÉ
A bidding style in which, with two suits, the shorter suit is bid first. The style was originally developed by Pierre Albarran in France and has influenced Italian bidding theory. It was incorporated in the Neapolitan Club, Blue Club and Roman systems. See BLUE CLUB, ROMAN SYSTEM.

CANSINO
Defense to a 1NT opening bid where an overcall of 2♣ shows clubs and two other suits, and a 2♦ overcall shows both majors. See DEFENSE TO 1NT.

CAPPELLETTI CUE-BIDS
Designed for use when the opponents have bid two suits. Each cue-bid shows length in both unbid suits. The cheaper cue-bid shows greater length in the lower-ranking unbid suit, while the more remote cue-bid shows greater length in the higher-ranking unbid sut.

CAPPELLETTI OVER NOTRUMP
A system of showing one-suited or two-suited hands over an opponent's opening bid of one notrump. Overcaller's two-level bids are largely artificial and have the following meanings:

2♣	=	any one-suited hand
2♦	=	hearts and spades
2♥	=	hearts and a minor suit
2♠	=	spades and a minor suit
2NT	=	clubs and diamonds

Cappelletti is also known as Hamilton or Jordan in various parts of the United States.

CAPTAINCY
The bidding principle whereby one partner is obliged to take responsibility for placing the contract once his partner's hand is limited in strength.

CARD(S)
Deck of 52 used to play bridge and other games, usually made of pasteboard.

CARD COMBINATIONS
See SUIT COMBINATION.

CARD READING
The ability to determine the distribution and location of key cards from the bidding and played cards.

CARD SENSE
An intangible quality that those skilled in card play seem to possess.

CARRY-OVER SCORE
When a tournament is played over more than one session, the carry-over score is that part of the score carried over from a previous session.

CARVE
Slang term meaning to misplay. "Butcher" and "Misere" are similar terms.

CASH
To lead a winning card or cards.

CASH OUT (CASH IN)
To take a series of tricks by leading winning cards. The term is usually applied to the situation when a player realizes that he is on lead for the last time and takes all the tricks that he can.

CHANGE OF SUIT
The bid of a different suit.

CHANGING A CALL
A slip of the tongue during the bidding, if corrected within the same breath, carries no penalty. An insufficient bid, if corrected to the proper level in the same denomination, is also allowable. But when an insufficient bid is identified and the perpetrator changes his call to something other than the lowest allowable call in the same denomination, this leads to bidding and possible lead penalties. The Director should be summoned immediately when a bidding accident occurs.

CHEAPER MINOR
(1) A convention similar to the Fishbein convention using a double by the player sitting directly over the preemptor as a penalty double, and uses the bid of the cheaper minor suit for takeout.

(2) Cheaper minor can also be used as a second negative after a strong 2♣ opening.

CHEAPEST BID
The most economical bid available to a player.

CHECKBACK STAYMAN
When the bidding has been opened with one of a suit and the opener rebids in notrump, "Checkback" is designed to explore whether or not the partnership has an eight card major suit fit.

CHEST YOUR CARDS
Hold them close to you, so opponents will not be able to view your hand.

CHICAGO
A form of rubber bridge whereby each rubber comprises exactly four hands with pre-determined vulnerability. On the first deal neither side is vulnerable and on the fourth both sides are. On the other two deals, by prior agreement, one side is vulnerable. Scoring is similar to rubber bridge but with bonuses for games replacing the rubber bonus. If a hand is passed out, it is redealt by the same player. See CHUKKER.

CHINESE FINESSE
A deceptive play intended to make an opponent think an honor lead is the higher of a sequence of honors. For example:

a)   A 4 3   b)   A 4 3

  K 8 6 2   J 10 7   K 8 6 2   10 7 5

            Q 9 5   Q J 9

If South, as declarer with hand a), judges that West holds the King he may lead the Queen (suggesting he holds the Jack) hoping it will not be covered. On hand b), West would be right not to cover since South could then finesse, holding J 9 over 10 7. See COVERING HONORS, FINESSE.

CHUKKER
A term for the four deals at Chicago bridge. The term is borrowed from polo. See CHICAGO.

CINCINNATI CARDING
A method of signaling that usually allows the partner of the opening leader both to discourage continuation of the suit and to indicate which shift is desired. The Cincinnati method uses UP-SIDE-DOWN SIGNALS to show attitude on opening lead.

CLAIM
Declarer makes a claim by placing his cards face up on the table and announcing that he will win one or more of the remaining tricks. Defender makes a claim by showing any or all of his cards to declarer and announcing he will win one or more of the remaining tricks. When a player makes a claim he should state his intended line of play. If he fails to do so and the claim is contested then a restriction on his play may be imposed. In duplicate, when there is a Director present, if a claim is disputed play ceases and the Director must be called to adjudicate.

CLEAR A SUIT
To force out by successive leads adversely held high cards and so establish winners in the suit.

CLOSED HAND
The hand of the declarer as distinct from the "open" hand, the dummy.

CLOSED ROOM
In head-to-head teams of four matches, the two pairs of a team usually play in different rooms. One of these rooms may be designated the closed room, the other the open room. Spectators may watch in the open room but may not enter the closed room.

CLUB
(1) The lowest-ranking of the 4 suits (2) The symbols (♣) on these 13 cards (3) A group of players who play bridge together, as a duplicate or rubber bridge club.

COFFEE-HOUSING
Indulging in unethical behavior in an attempt to mislead the opponents. For example:

```
            K J
     Q 2          A 3
            5 4
```

On the lead of a small card from South, who is playing the contract, West pauses for thought before playing low, as he would if he held the Ace instead of the Queen, thus misleading declarer. The term originates from a style of bridge that used to be played in European coffee houses. See ALCATRAZ COUP.

COLD
Slang term describing a contract that is certain to be made. "Frigid" and "Icy" are similar terms.

COLDER THAN A CREEK (CRICK) ROCK
Slang for a very certain contract. See COLD.

COMBINATION FINESSE

A finesse intending to win a trick immediately or to set the stage for a winning finesse on the ensuing lead of the suit. A double finesse is a combination finesse:

A J 10

5 4 3

South leads a low card and inserts the ten from dummy if no honor appears from West. This will likely lose to an honor in East's hand. Hopefully the second finesse will work, as South re-enters his hand in some other suit and releads the suit to dummy's jack.

COME-ON

An encouraging attitude signal.

Communications

COMMUNICATIONS

The ability to transfer the lead between the two hands of a partnership.

COMPASS POINTS

North - South - East - West indicate the positions of players at the table.

COMPETITIVE AUCTION (COMPETITIVE BIDDING)

Bidding sequences in which both partnerships enter the auction.

COMPETITIVE DOUBLE(S)
A double, primarily for take out, but conveying the message that the bidder is unwilling to pass but has no satisfactory descriptive bid to make. See DOUBLE.

COMPOUND SQUEEZE
An elaborate, highly-involved squeeze position in which the declarer combines (in this order) a triple squeeze with a double squeeze. For instance:

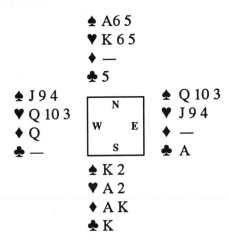

♠ A6 5
♥ K 6 5
♦ —
♣ 5

♠ J 9 4
♥ Q 10 3
♦ Q
♣ —

♠ Q 10 3
♥ J 9 4
♦ —
♣ A

♠ K 2
♥ A 2
♦ A K
♣ K

In a diamond contract, when South leads the ace of diamonds he puts pressure on East who must shed a major suit card when dummy discards a club. Then South leads the suit which East has discarded, first to the high card in dummy and then to the high card in his hand. Finally, the last diamond from South effects a double squeeze. West is squeezed in the majors and East in a major and clubs.

COMPUTER DEAL (COMPUTER HANDS)
(COMPUTER SCORING)
Term to describe the dealing of hands by computer. These hands are commonly used in tournaments and other competitions of more than one section.

CONCEDE
To give one or more tricks to the opposition.

CONCESSION
A player makes a concession when he announces he will lose the remaining tricks or agrees to a claim by the opposition. See CLAIM.

CONDONE
To bid or play immediately following an irregularity and thereby convert it into a legal action.

CONGRESS
(British) A tournament, typically played over a (long) weekend, and often comprising several competitions.

CONSTRUCTIVE
Description of a bid which is helpful and forward going.

CONSTRUCTIVE BIDDING
Auctions in which one side tries to reach its best contract without interference.

CONTRACT(ING)
The undertaking by declarer to win the number of tricks, in the denomination named, specified by the final bid of the auction.

CONTRACT BRIDGE
Contract Bridge evolved slowly from the game of Whist, through the games of Auction Whist, Auction Bridge and finally to Contract Bridge in 1926. It differed from its predecessors in that only tricks bid for and made counted towards game (based on the Plafond system). The method of scoring was changed considerably by Harold Vanderbilt who perfected the new game with the inclusion of incentives for games and slams, as well as the Plafond system of bidding towards game by accumulating partscores.

CONTROL
A holding in a suit that prevents opponents cashing more than a certain number of tricks in the suit. An Ace or void (in a suit contract) constitutes a first round control, a King or singleton (in a suit contract) constitutes a second round control. In some systems, notably the Blue Club, Aces and Kings are given numerical values: Aces two, Kings one. Responses to the strong 1♣ opening show how many controls are held.

CONTROL ASKING BIDS
These elicit specific information in a particular suit or suits concerning first, second or even third round control. The captain in the auction is usually the stronger hand and the other partner supplies the answer(s).

CONTROLLED PSYCHES
A psychic bid is one which deliberately violates a partnership agreement. A psychic bid which can be controlled by some special bid by partner is called a controlled psyche and makes the use of such bids safer. See PSYCHIC BID.

Conventions

CONVENTION
A call or play with a defined meaning understood by the partnership, possibly with little similarity to the natural use of the bid. See ALERT.

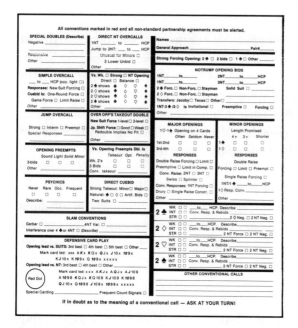

CONVENTION CARD

A form on which both members of a partnership give details of the system of bidding they are using and their methods of leads, discards and signals. It varies from the simple, acceptable in most local clubs, to the very detailed information which is required by sponsoring organizations for major tournaments. The opposite side can be used for recording scores. Also called a personal score card or private score.

COOPERATIVE DOUBLES

A double that gives the doubler's partner the choice of passing for penalties or bidding on. They are used principally at low levels of the auction.

COUNT

The defensive carding system by which partners indicate the number of cards they hold in a suit. High-low shows an even number of cards and low-high indicates an odd number. This may be done when discarding or following suit (or in some systems, even when leading, i.e. third and fifth best leads).

COUNT SIGNALS
A signal to convey information about the length of a suit rather than its strength. In standard methods a high-low shows an even number of cards.

COUNTING ONE'S CARDS
The Laws of Duplicate Contract Bridge state that each player should count his cards, before he looks at his hand, to check that he has thirteen. They also require that the cards be recounted at the end of play before being replaced in the board.

Counting a Hand

COUNTING (OUT) A HAND
This refers to either high cards or distribution, and may be done by either declarer or defender.

1) High cards: subtract the high card points a player has already produced during the play of a hand from the number of points he promised during the bidding. The remainder should equal the number of points (high cards) still in his hand.

2) Distribution: Subtract the number of cards in each suit (shown by the player through the bidding or the play) in three of the suits from thirteen. The remainder equals the number of cards in the fourth suit held by that player.

COUP

A specialized maneuver during the play of the hand. Many coups are given identifying names, some descriptive, others from the names of their authors or the places where they first surfaced. See ALCATRAZ COUP, BATH COUP, COUP EN PASSANT, CROCODILE COUP, DESCHAPELLES COUP, DEVIL'S COUP, GRAND COUP, MERRIMAC COUP, MORTON'S FORK COUP, SCISSORS COUP, TRUMP COUP, VIENNA COUP.

COUP EN PASSANT

The lead of a plain suit card to promote a low trump sitting over a high trump. For example:

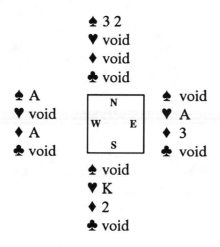

♠ 3 2
♥ void
♦ void
♣ void

♠ A   ♠ void
♥ void   ♥ A
♦ A   ♦ 3
♣ void   ♣ void

♠ void
♥ K
♦ 2
♣ void

In the diagram above, with hearts as trumps, a spade is led from the North hand. If East discards, South ruffs and, if East ruffs, South's King is promoted as a winner. See TRUMP PROMOTION.

COUP WITHOUT A NAME

Also known as the Scissors Coup. This is a play designed to cut the defenders' communications, to prevent a ruff.

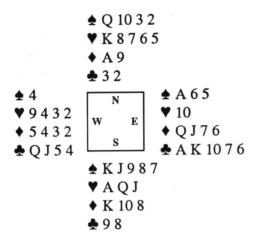

```
              ♠ Q 10 3 2
              ♥ K 8 7 6 5
              ♦ A 9
              ♣ 3 2
  ♠ 4                      ♠ A 6 5
  ♥ 9 4 3 2      N         ♥ 10
  ♦ 5 4 3 2    W   E       ♦ Q J 7 6
  ♣ Q J 5 4      S         ♣ A K 10 7 6
              ♠ K J 9 8 7
              ♥ A Q J
              ♦ K 10 8
              ♣ 9 8
```

RHO opens the bidding with one club but your side prevails at four spades. LHO leads the queen of clubs, but RHO overtakes with his king of clubs and switches to a very sinister-looking ten of hearts. If you try to attack trumps, RHO will win the ace, underlead his club to partner's queen and obtain a heart ruff. To counter this, declarer leads three rounds of diamonds and discards dummy's last club on the third round. Now the communications have been severed and West cannot obtain the lead to give partner the anticipated ruff.

COURTESY BID

A response made on minimum values to an opening bid, in case opener is very strong, is sometimes called a courtesy bid.

COVERING HONORS

The maxim "Cover an honor with an honor" coming from the early days of whist is usually sound bridge technique, but there are exceptions. See CHINESE FINESSE.

CRACK (CRACK IT)
To make a penalty double.

CRASH
Based on a series of two-suited overcalls in defense against a strong, artificial one club opening. The name CRASH comes from the mnemonic device reflecting the pertinent characteristic of the suit pairs announced by the one diamond, one heart and one notrump bids. In that order, the overcalls show **C**olor, **RA**nk, and **SH**ape.

1♦ = two suits of the same color

1♥ = two suits of the same rank, i.e., either both majors or both minors

1NT = two suits, both of which either have rounded tops (i.e., clubs and hearts) or pointed tops (i.e., diamonds and spades).

Crashing Honors

CRASHING HONORS
The playing of two high honors by defenders to the same trick. A deceptive play by declarer can sometimes induce defenders to crash their honors. For example:

```
            Q 5 4 3 2
    A                   K 6
            J 10 9 8 7
```

If South, declarer, leads the Queen from dummy, East may decide to cover causing the defenders to crash their honors.

CRISP VALUES
Aces and Kings.

CRISS-CROSS SQUEEZE
Thought by many to be the most fun of all the squeezes, this squeeze operates against either opponent holding the second highest card in two suits.

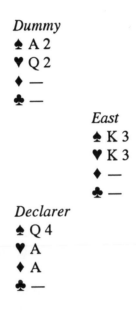

Dummy
♠ A 2
♥ Q 2
♦ —
♣ —

East
♠ K 3
♥ K 3
♦ —
♣ —

Declarer
♠ Q 4
♥ A
♦ A
♣ —

When declarer leads his ace of diamonds and discards the low spade from the dummy, East is finished. No matter which major suit he discards, declarer simply cashes the ace of that suit and then crosses to the other ace to score the queen of East's discarded suit. Note that if the East-West hands were interchanged, the squeeze would still operate.

CROCODILE COUP

A play by a defender of an apparently unnecessarily high card to prevent his partner from being thrown in. The defender can be imagined as a crocodile opening its jaws in order to make certain that it catches partner's winning card (which by this stage is a singleton). For example:

```
            ♠ 3 2
            ♥ A Q
♠ A Q                   ♠ K
♥ 7 6                   ♥ K 5 4
            ♠ 5 4
            ♥ 3 2
```

If South, declarer, leads a spade, West must play his Ace swallowing his partner's King, in order to prevent East from winning and having to lead into the heart tenace.

CROSSRUFF

A play in which trumps in both hands are used to ruff losers rather than draw trumps. It is usually correct to play off the side suit winners before starting to crossruff to prevent opponents discarding those suits and later being in a position to ruff declarer's winners.

CROWHURST

A convention whereby a response of 2♣ by responder to a wide range 1NT rebid by opener is an enquiry. For example, if the 1NT rebid by opener shows 12 - 16 points then the responses after 1♥ - Pass - 1♠ - Pass - 1NT - Pass - 2♣ would be as follows:

    2♦   12 - 14 points without 5 hearts or 3 spades.
    2♥   12 - 14 points with 5 hearts.
    2♠   12 - 14 points with 3 spades.
    2NT 15 - 16 points.

CUE BID

Basically this is a bid of a suit with no intention that the bid suit should be considered as the trump suit. The term is used to cover several quite different situations. When the possibility of a slam is being investigated and the trump suit has been agreed (either explicitly or implicitly), then the cue bid of a suit shows a control in that suit. By partnership agreement this may be first round control (an Ace or void), or either first or second round control. (See ADVANCE CUE BID, SPLINTER BID). In a contested auction the cue bid of an opponent's suit may be used as a general forcing bid (when no suitable alternative is available) or to convey a specific message or request. (See DIRECTIONAL ASKING BID, UNASSUMING CUE BID). When an opponent's opening bid is directly overcalled in the same suit the message conveyed is either a very powerful hand or, more popularly, some form of two-suited hand. (See MICHAELS CUE BID).

After the last rubber of the "Battle of the Century," (see page 19) Sidney Lenz congratulates Josephine Culbertson. Left to right: Cmdr. Winfield Liggett Jr., Lenz, Oswald Jacoby, Theodore Lightner, Mrs. Culbertson, Ely Culbertson, and Lt. Al Gruenther, referee.

CULBERTSON SYSTEM

System of bidding devised and popularized by Ely Culbertson, first published in the Blue Book in 1933 and later revised in further Blue Books. Many of the features of the Culbertson system have provided a basis for modern methods. The system was influenced by the very successful Four Aces team and by public opinion, leading to the publication of the Gold Book in 1936 which became standard in America for nearly fifteen years. Features of the system were: 1) Valuation by Honor Tricks, 2) Uniform standards for biddable suits, 3) The approach forcing principle, 4) Forcing two bids, 5) The forcing take out showing three Honor Tricks, 6) Strong no trump, 7) Non-forcing jump rebids by opener unless in a new suit, 8) Asking bids.

CULBERTSON 4 - 5NT

A slam convention showing Aces and Kings as well as asking for them. The 4NT bid shows three Aces or two Aces and a King of a suit bid by the partnership. The responses are: With two Aces or one Ace and a King of a suit bid by the partnership, bid 5NT. Holding no Ace, bid five of the lowest suit that has been bid by the partnership. Holding one Ace, bid the suit with the Ace at the five level, or at the six level if it is the Ace of the lowest suit genuinely bid by the partnership.

CURSE OF SCOTLAND

Name given to the nine of diamonds. Various explanations have been suggested: 1) In the game Pope Joan the nine of diamonds was called the Pope, the Antichrist of Scotland. 2) In the game Cornette, introduced to Scotland by the unfortunate Mary Queen of Scots, the nine of diamonds was the chief card. 3) "Butcher" Cumberland wrote the orders for the Battle of Culloden (1746) on the card. 4) The order for the massacre at Glencoe was signed on the back of the card. 5) That it is derived from the nine lozenges that formed the arms of the Earl of Star, who was hated for his part in the massacre at Glencoe and the union with England.

CURTAIN CARD

(British) Written record of a hand in a duplicate board which can be used to restore the hand if the board is fouled. See HAND RECORDS.

CUT

1) Before the beginning of a rubber a deck of cards is spread face down on the table and each player draws one card. Those drawing the two highest cards partner each other.

2) Before every deal the deck is cut, towards the dealer, by dividing it into two portions. The lower portion is replaced on top of the other.

3) To ruff.

4) The place at which the field is divided in a qualifying session to decide who goes forward to the next stage.

CUT IN

In rubber bridge, the draw for partners. In a club, it distinguishes a session when members can turn up and draw for random partners for each rubber from one in which two players partner each other for the whole time.

CUT THROAT BRIDGE

A version of three-handed bridge.

DAB

An acronym for "**D**irectional **A**sking **B**id." See DIRECTIONAL ASKING BID.

DANGER HAND

During the play of a contract, it can be dangerous to lose the lead to one opponent but safe to lose it to the other. The hand that declarer needs to prevent gaining the lead is termed the danger hand. Sometimes declarer can organize life accordingly. For example:

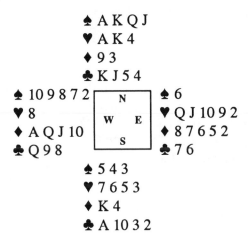

```
              ♠ A K Q J
              ♥ A K 4
              ♦ 9 3
              ♣ K J 5 4
♠ 10 9 8 7 2      N        ♠ 6
♥ 8          W       E     ♥ Q J 10 9 2
♦ A Q J 10                 ♦ 8 7 6 5 2
♣ Q 9 8          S         ♣ 7 6
              ♠ 5 4 3
              ♥ 7 6 5 3
              ♦ K 4
              ♣ A 10 3 2
```

Playing in 3NT, South receives the lead of the spade 10. He has eight top tricks and can develop a ninth in clubs. He has a two-way finesse available in the suit. He should however finesse the 10 so that, if the finesse loses, West, the safe hand, is on lead. Should East gain the lead a diamond switch could, as here, be fatal.

DATUM

(British) The average score obtained on a board in an event with Butler scoring. In a large field the top and bottom scores are ignored to give a more representative score. Each individual result is compared to the datum and converted to I.M.Ps. See BUTLER METHOD, INTERNATIONAL MATCH POINTS (I.M.P.s).

DEAD

A player is dead if he has no successful recourse. A dummy is dead if it is entryless.

DEAL

1) To distribute the 52 cards, one card to each player in turn starting with the player on the left of the dealer.

2) The set of 4 hands dealt.

DEALER

The person who deals.

DECEPTIVE PLAY (DECEPTIVE LEAD)

The play of a card, or a line of play, with the express intention of deceiving opponents about the true lie of the cards.

DECK

A pack of playing cards.

DECLARATION

The final contract.

DECLARER
The player who first bid the denomination of the final contract.

Declarer

DEEP FINESSE
A finesse against several cards, in the hope of establishing extra tricks in the suit. For example:

A 10 9 8

4 3 2

Needing two tricks in the suit, and with entries to hand available, if South plays three times towards North's holding and finesses each time, he will make two tricks provided West holds an honor. See FINESSE.

DEFEAT THE CONTRACT
On defense, to win enough tricks so that declarer cannot make his contract even if he wins all the remaining tricks.

DEFENDERS
    1) During the auction, the non-opening side.
    2) During the play, the non-declaring side.

DEFENSE, THE
1) The two defenders.
2) The line of play adopted by the defenders.

DEFENSE TO ARTIFICIAL STRONG CLUB
Term given to a partnership agreement about entering the bidding after an opponent's strong artificial 1♣ opening bid.

DEFENSE TO 1NT
Term given to a partnership agreement about entering the bidding after an opponent's 1NT opening bid. See ASPRO, ASTRO, CANSINO, LANDY, RIPSTRA, SHARPLES.

DEFENSE TO OPENING THREE BID
Term given to partnership agreement about entering the bidding after an opponent's preemptive three level opening bid. See FILM, FISHBEIN, FOXU, LOWER MINOR, OPTIONAL DOUBLE.

DEFENSIVE BIDDING
Bidding by the non-opening side, sometimes with an obstructive intent.

DEFENSIVE TRICK
A card combination which wins a trick in defense.

DELAYED GAME RAISE
When partner opens one of a major suit and the responder has values for game, it is valuable to distinguish between hands with distributional values and hands with trump support and all round strength (usually 13 to 15 points). In the first case a direct raise to game, which has the additional value of having a pre-emptive effect, is in order. In the second case the nature of the hand is best described by bidding a second suit and then bidding game in partner's opening suit at the next opportunity — a delayed game raise.

DELAYED STAYMAN
See CHECKBACK STAYMAN.

DELAYED SUPPORT
An invitational raise in partner's first bid suit on the second round of bidding usually showing three card support as in the sequence: 1♥ - Pass - 2♣ - Pass - 2♦ - Pass - 3♥.

DELTA SUIT ASKING BIDS
In the Super Precision System, after a notrump response to a one club opening, the opener can ask about the number of cards and honors the responder has in a specific suit. He asks by jumping in a new suit.

DEMAND BID
Any forcing bid.

DENIAL BID
A bid that indicates lack of support for partner's suit, or general weakness such as the 2♦ response to an Acol 2♣ opening. See HERBERT NEGATIVE, NEGATIVE RESPONSE.

DENOMINATIONS
Clubs, diamonds, hearts, spades or no trumps.

DEPO
Convention handling intervention after a Blackwood 4NT bid. The name is a mnemonic for "Double Even Pass Odd." A double after intervention shows zero, two or four Aces, the pass shows one or three.

DESCHAPELLES COUP
Defensive play involving the sacrifice of a high card in order to gain entry to partner's hand. For example:

A 5

Q 6 4   K 8 7 3

J 10 9 2

Requiring an entry into partner's hand, East makes the Deschapelles coup by leading the King. If South, the declarer, takes the King with dummy's Ace, the Queen is now an entry, and if declarer ducks the King, East simply leads another card establishing an extra trick.

DEUCE
The two spot of a suit.

DEVIL'S BEDPOST
Bridge jargon for the four of clubs.

DEVIL'S COUP

A coup whereby a seemingly certain trump loser vanishes. For example:

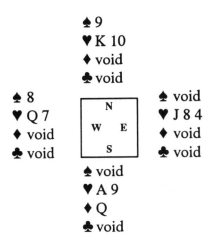

```
              ♠ 9
              ♥ K 10
              ♦ void
              ♣ void
♠ 8                          ♠ void
♥ Q 7          N             ♥ J 8 4
♦ void     W       E         ♦ void
♣ void         S             ♣ void
              ♠ void
              ♥ A 9
              ♦ Q
              ♣ void
```

Hearts are trumps, and South, declarer, leads the nine of spades from dummy. East trumps, and South overtrumps. If East plays the Jack, South ruffs with the Ace, and finesses the 10 of hearts. If East trumps with a lower card, South ruffs with the 9 and takes the top two trumps for the final two tricks.

DEVIL'S PICTURE BOOK
Name given to playing cards by English Puritans.

DEVYN PRESS
The largest American bridge publisher. A division of Baron Barclay Bridge Supplies.

D.I. ("Declarative Interrogative" or "Declarative Informatory")

A four notrump bid that is not natural and does not ask how many aces are held, but rather asks partner to show a previously undisclosed feature.

DIAMOND

(1)The second-lowest ranking suit (2) The symbol (♦) of this suit.

DIRECTION

North, South, East or West.

DIRECTIONAL ASKING BID (DAB)

After an overcall, a cue bid of the enemy suit by the opening side asks partner to bid no trumps if he holds a partial stopper in the suit bid by the opposition. See CUE BID.

DIRECTOR

See TOURNAMENT DIRECTOR.

DISCARD(ING)

A card played to a trick which is not of the suit led and not the trump suit.

DISCOURAGING BID

A bid showing a poor holding for a particular auction; an attempt to slow partner's enthusiasm for bidding further.

DISCOURAGING CARD

A card signalling the fact that a defender does not wish a suit to be continued or led. See ATTITUDE SIGNALS.

DISCOVERY PLAY

A declarer who tests the distribution of the outstanding cards in the unseen hands before committing himself to one line of play is said to be making a discovery play.

DISTRIBUTION
The lie of the cards.

DISTRIBUTIONAL POINT COUNT
Points based on distribution which can be added to the High Card Point value of a hand in order to improve the estimation of its playing strength. A number of methods are in use, some based on shortages, others on length. For example:

1) The Goren Count (or 3-2-1 count) adds three points for a void, two for a singleton and one for a doubleton.

2) The Karpin Count adds points not for shortages, but for extra length in the bid suit, one extra point for each card over four in the longest suit; so a five card suit gains one point, a six card suit gains two extra points. The Karpin count is used by opener in evaluating his hand. In responding, with primary trump support, the 5-3-1 count is more accurate while the 3-2-1 count is used with only secondary support.

While the shortage and length points methods produce similar results, both may be improved somewhat with the following additions:

With a singleton King, Queen or Jack, deduct one point.
With five trumps in the responding hand, add one point.
See POINT COUNT, POINTS.

DISTRIBUTIONAL VALUE
A holding of worth due to shortage or length in suits. See DISTRIBUTIONAL POINT COUNT.

DISTRICT (ACBL)
The ACBL is made up of twenty-five geographically designated Districts which are represented on the ACBL Board of Directors and the ACBL Board of Governors. Each District also has responsibility for scheduling and running its allotted Regional Tournaments and overseeing the scheduling of Sectional Tournaments of its member Units. See A.C.B.L.

DOG
Slang for a poor hand.

DOOP
A one table (4 person) bridge game that uses computer dealt hands from Regional and National tournaments. The players bid, play and compare their results.

DOPE / ROPE
Conventions used after intervention following a Blackwood 4NT, allowing responder to show an even number of Aces or an odd number of Aces. After an intervening bid, <u>D</u>ouble shows an <u>O</u>dd number of Aces, <u>P</u>ass an <u>E</u>ven number. After an intervening double, <u>R</u>edouble shows an <u>O</u>dd number of Aces and <u>P</u>ass an <u>E</u>ven number. It is usually used at the 6 or 7 level when there is not enough room to use DOPI or ROPI.

DOPI / ROPI
Conventions used after intervention following a Blackwood 4NT. Following an intervening bid, <u>D</u>ouble shows zero (<u>O</u>) Aces, <u>P</u>ass one (<u>I</u>) and other responses on a step principle, the first step (e.g. 5♥ after a 5♦ overcall) showing two Aces etc. After an intervening double, <u>R</u>edouble shows zero (<u>O</u>) Aces, <u>P</u>ass one (<u>I</u>) Ace etc.

OH DEAR, NOW WE *DID* DISCUSS THIS... IS THAT FOR TAKE*OUT* OR PENALTY?...

DOUBLE

A call that increases the value of tricks bid and made, the penalty for undertricks, the bonuses for overtricks and will lead to an additional bonus of 50 points if the doubled contract is successful. The call is used conventionally for several purposes. See COMPETITIVE DOUBLE, DOUBLE OF THREE NO TRUMP BIDS, LIGHTNER DOUBLE, NEGATIVE DOUBLE, PENALTY DOUBLE, RESPONSIVE DOUBLE, TAKE OUT DOUBLE, UNPENALTY DOUBLE.

DOUBLE-BARRELLED STAYMAN
See TWO WAY STAYMAN.

DOUBLE COUP

Ruffing twice to reduce trumps sufficiently to execute a trump coup:

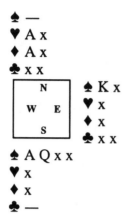

♠ —
♥ A x
♦ A x
♣ x x

♠ K x
♥ x
♦ x
♣ x x

♠ A Q x x
♥ x
♦ x
♣ —

Spades are trump. With the lead in dummy, declarer leads a club and ruffs. Returning to dummy with a red ace, declarer ruffs another club. Back to dummy with the other red ace and East's king of trump is couped.

DOUBLE DUMMY

A play in a particular situation which could not possibly be bettered even if declarer could see all four hands. To examine a hand double dummy is to look at all four hands simultaneously. A double dummy problem is one in which all four hands are displayed.

DOUBLE FINESSE

A finesse against two outstanding honors. For example:

A Q 10
K J 8   9 7 6 2
5 4 3

South must first finesse the 10, and then the Queen to take all three tricks. See FINESSE, REPEATED FINESSE.

DOUBLE JUMP
Skipping two levels in the bidding (1♣ - 3♦ / 3♥ / 3♠ or 1♣ - 4♣).

DOUBLE JUMP OVERCALL
An overcall skipping two levels (e.g. 1♥ - 3♠).

DOUBLE JUMP RAISE
A raise missing two levels of bidding. It is usually pre-emptive in nature.

DOUBLE NEGATIVE
In the sequence 2♣ - Pass - 2♦ - Pass - 2♥ / 2♠ - Pass - 2NT some partnerships agree that the 2NT bid is a second negative, showing a very poor hand.

DOUBLE OF THREE NO TRUMP BIDS
When the opponents bid to 3NT a double by the defender who will not be on lead is usually played as lead directing asking for a particular lead, often dummy's first bid suit. If both defenders have bid a different suit, the double asks partner to lead his own suit rather than that of the doubler. If no suit has been bid a double shows a long solid suit and asks partner to lead his shortest suit. See DOUBLE.

DOUBLE RAISE
A raise of opener's suit by two levels (e.g. 1♠ - Pass - 3♠). In many modern systems, it is a limit raise usually showing four card support and 10 - 12 points. See INVERTED MINOR SUIT RAISES.

DOUBLE SQUEEZE
See SQUEEZE.

DOUBLED INTO GAME
A contract which undoubled would not be a game bid but because of the double will make game should it succeed.

DOUBLER
The person who doubles.

DOUBLETON
A holding of two cards in a suit.

DOWN
Having made fewer tricks than contracted for.

DRAWING TRUMP(S)
The act of playing successive rounds of trumps in order to extract opposing trumps.

Drawing Trump(s)

DRIVE OUT
To force out an opponent's high card by leading a sufficiently high card in the same suit and continuing the suit until the outstanding high card is played.

DROP
Cause a missing high card to fall by playing a still higher card or cards.

DRURY
A conventional 2♣ response to a third or fourth hand opening asking if the opener has a sound or sub-minimum opener.

DUCK(DUCKING)
To decline to take a trick that one could have won.

DUKE OF CUMBERLAND'S HAND

Dealt to the son of George IV at whist. Clubs were trumps and the Duke held:

♠ A K Q ♥ A K Q J ♦ A K ♣ K J 9 7

His opponents bet that he would not make a single trick in his hand. According to the story, he accepted the bet and lost all thirteen tricks. The complete deal was:

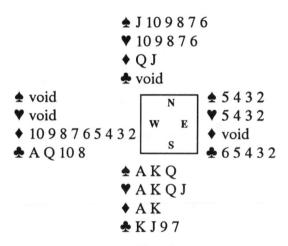

```
                  ♠ J 10 9 8 7 6
                  ♥ 10 9 8 7 6
                  ♦ Q J
                  ♣ void
    ♠ void          ┌─────────┐      ♠ 5 4 3 2
    ♥ void          │    N    │      ♥ 5 4 3 2
    ♦ 10 9 8 7 6 5 4 3 2  W   E      ♦ void
    ♣ A Q 10 8      │    S    │      ♣ 6 5 4 3 2
                  └─────────┘
                  ♠ A K Q
                  ♥ A K Q J
                  ♦ A K
                  ♣ K J 9 7
```

Following whist principles of the time, the Duke led the 7 of clubs. The lead was won with the 8, and after two diamond ruffs and two further club leads through the Duke, the last trump was drawn and the seven remaining diamonds cashed.

DUMB BIDDER

(British) Device to permit silent bidding. It is a board placed in the center of the table, subdivided into labelled regions, 1♣, 1♦, 1♥, 1♠, 1NT, 2♣ etc. (up to 7NT), **DBL, RDBL, ALERT, STOP** and **NO BID**. A player makes his call by touching the appropriate region of the board with a pen or pencil or moving a small coin placed on the dumb bidder.

DUMMY

    1) The partner of the declarer.

    2) The hand of the partner of the declarer.

DUMMY REVERSAL

A method of playing a hand such that trumps in the longer hand (declarer's) are used to ruff dummy's losers. Dummy's trumps are then used to draw the remaining trumps. Here is an example:

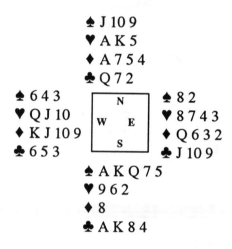

```
              ♠ J 10 9
              ♥ A K 5
              ♦ A 7 5 4
              ♣ Q 7 2
  ♠ 6 4 3        N        ♠ 8 2
  ♥ Q J 10              ♥ 8 7 4 3
  ♦ K J 10 9  W     E   ♦ Q 6 3 2
  ♣ 6 5 3        S        ♣ J 10 9
              ♠ A K Q 7 5
              ♥ 9 6 2
              ♦ 8
              ♣ A K 8 4
```

South is in a contract of 7♠, but has only eleven top tricks. Declarer can get home however, if the black suits break evenly, with a dummy reversal play. If dummy's three losing diamonds are ruffed with declarer's top trumps, South ends up with three trump tricks, four club tricks, three tricks from the red suit winners and three tricks by trumping diamonds in hand. If the hand is looked at as a problem of disposing of dummy's losers, it is then obvious that the solution is to ruff the three diamond losers and dispose of the heart loser on the fourth club.

DUMMY'S RIGHTS
Dummy has specific rights and obligations in duplicate and rubber bridge which are discussed in detail in the Laws.

Dummy's Rights.

DUOBRIDGE
A four-handed bridge game for 2 players.

DUPLICATE BRIDGE
A form of bridge in which each board is played several times by different players. The luck of the deal is thus eliminated since players' scores are compared with the other results on each board. The first application of the duplicate principle was in Duplicate Whist by John T. Mitchell, inventor of the first pairs movement. Duplicate Auction Bridge was first played in 1914 under the auspices of the American Whist League.

DUPLICATION OF DISTRIBUTION
A duplication of distribution is said to occur when both players have exactly the same length in each suit. It is also called "Mirror distribution."

DUPLICATION OF VALUES
A duplication of values is said to occur when both players have a strong holding in a particular suit. Therefore, although during the auction there may appear to be many points between the two hands, the combined trick taking ability is limited.

DYNAMIC ONE NOTRUMP

An integral part of the Romex system. It is a strong opening bid showing a relatively unbalanced hand and 18 to 21 points, including at least five controls.

EAST
One of the positions at the bridge table.

EASTERN SCIENTIFIC
A bidding system featuring five-card majors with a forcing notrump, strong notrump openings, strong two club openings, weak two bids, negative doubles and other gadgets.

ECHO
The play of an unnecessarily high card on the first round of a suit and a lower card on the second round as a method of signalling. It is also known as a "High-Low" signal or a "Peter."

ECONOMY OF HONORS
During the play, the practice of trying to protect and conserve honors from the opponents' trumps or honors.

EHAA (Every Hand An Adventure)
A natural system featuring 10-12 notrump opening, 4 card majors and very undisiplined weak two bids in all 4 suits (6-12 HCP, 5+ cards in the suit and almost any distribution).

ELEVEN, RULE OF
See RULE OF ELEVEN.

ELIMINATION (PLAY)
The process of removing neutral cards from defenders' hands in order that they have no useful lead when they are thrown in (given the lead).

ELOPEMENT
Making off with tricks using trumps that are not high. See COUP EN PASSANT.

EMPTY
Small cards instead of honors, as in "King empty fourth," Kxxx.

EN PASSANT
See COUP EN PASSANT.

ENCOURAGING
A term applied to a bid or card which urges partner to continue.

ENCRYPTED SIGNALS
Signals based on information which is available to both defenders, but not to declarer.

ENDPLAY
A term used when an opponent is given the lead at a vital stage of the play and, with his subsequent lead, is forced to concede a trick or tricks and is therefore "endplayed". The vital point is more likely to occur in the end stage of the play.

ENTRY
1) A card that can be used to enter a particular hand.

2) Seating assignment sold to each player, pair or team at a club or tournament.

ENTRY KILLING PLAY
A defensive maneuver designed to destroy entries either in declarer's hand or in dummy. See MERRIMAC COUP, SCISSORS COUP.

ENTRY SQUEEZE

Forces a defender to discard an apparently meaningless card (not a winner, not even protection for a winner), but in so doing creates an extra entry for declarer. Here is an example from "Adventures in Card Play."

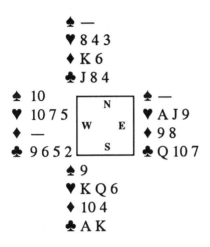

```
              ♠ —
              ♥ 8 4 3
              ♦ K 6
              ♣ J 8 4
♠ 10                        ♠ —
♥ 10 7 5      ┌─────┐       ♥ A J 9
              │  N  │
♦ —           │W   E│       ♦ 9 8
              │  S  │
♣ 9 6 5 2     └─────┘       ♣ Q 10 7
              ♠ 9
              ♥ K Q 6
              ♦ 10 4
              ♣ A K
```

South is on lead at notrump. With only the king of diamonds as an entry to lead towards the KQ6 of hearts it appears South can take only five tricks. If South could create another entry to dummy a second heart trick would be gained. The lead of the nine of spades does just that. West wins but East has a problem. A club discard is silly and a heart would allow South to make two heart tricks. But those "meaningless" diamonds could easily be spared. Not so, for then South could overtake the ten of diamonds with the king and the six of diamonds would be the second entry.

EQUALS

A holding of cards in sequence at the start of play, or of the same value as the play progresses, is said to be a holding of "equals."

ESCAPE MECHANISM
A bidding device used to locate the safest fit after the opponents have doubled for penalties. Often applied after the double of a weak or mini no trump opening.

Escape Mechanism

ESCAPE SUIT
A suit held in reserve by a player making a psychic bid. For a regular systemic bid with an escape suit. See GAMBLING 3NT.

ESTABLISH
To force out (or otherwise remove) the high cards stopping a suit being cashed. For example:

K Q J

4 3 2

The Ace of the suit needs to be forced out in order to establish two tricks in the suit.

ESTABLISHED CARD
A card that has been established.

ESTABLISHED ENTRY
An entry which has been established.

ESTABLISHED REVOKE
A revoke becomes established (i.e. it cannot be corrected) when one of the offending side leads or plays to the next trick. A revoke on the twelfth trick cannot be established.

ESTABLISHED SUIT
A suit is said to have been established if it can be cashed.

ESTIMATE
Try to keep track of the score during a duplicate or team game.

Estimate

ETHICAL CONDUCT
Proper behavior which stresses fair play.

ETHICS
The Proprieties of the game as distinct from the actual Laws.

ETIQUETTE
In general, good manners at the bridge table. (For example, declarer thanking partner when dummy is faced).

EVEN
    1) Term applied to an even division of the outstanding cards (3 - 3 is the even break with six cards outstanding; 4 - 3 an even distribution of seven).

    2) An even card is one with an even number of pips (2, 4, 6 etc.).

EXCLUSION BID

A bid showing length in all suits other than the one named. A takeout double is a form of exclusion bid. In the Roman System, a player clarifies his 2♣ or 2♦ opener (both bids showing three-suited hands) by bidding his short suit at his second call.

EXHAUST

To draw all the outstanding cards in a suit from a particular hand.

EXIT

To surrender the lead.

EXIT CARD

A card used to exit in the hope of a favorable return. See THROW IN.

Expert

EXPERT

A player universally (or locally) appreciated for his skill at the game of bridge.

EXPLANATION OF BID

If a player is asked to explain his partner's bid, he should fully explain the partnership agreement according to the system being played. It is wrong to offer an explanation of what the bid ought to mean, or to say how one proposes to interpret it. If the partnership has no agreement (explicit or implicit) then the player should say so. An explanation must not be offered unless opponents ask.

EXPOSED CARD

A card wrongly or inadvertently exposed during the auction or play. The Laws apply.

EXPOSED HAND

1) The dummy.

2) Declarer or a defender may expose their hand when making a claim.

EXTENDED STAYMAN

After a 2♦ response to the 2♣ enquiry, a further enquiry bid of 3♦ asks about three card major suits. In reply:

3♥   Shows three hearts and two spades.
3♠   Shows three spades and two hearts.
3NT   Shows two spades and two hearts.
4♣   Shows three cards in both majors.

See STAYMAN CONVENTION.

EXTRA TRICK

Overtrick; a trick scored in excess of the number of tricks required to fulfill a contract.

FACE
To turn a card so that its front is visible to the other players. See FACED LEAD, BOXED.

FACE CARD
Any jack, queen or king (because these cards have faces on them).

FACED LEAD
In duplicate bridge the opening lead must be made face down. This is to allow partner to ask questions regarding the auction without influencing the choice of lead. When these questions are completed the card is turned over or "faced." See FACE.

FACTORING
The process of adjusting a matchpoint score. If, for example, some pairs have played fewer boards than the rest of the field then their scores must be factored up by the appropriate fraction. Alternatively, the scores of the pairs playing more boards may be factored down. See MATCHPOINT(S).

FALL OF THE CARDS
The disposition of the cards as ordained by fate.

FALSE CARDING (FALSE CARD)
Deceptive play of a card in the hope that the opposition will misread the holding in the suit.

FALSE PREFERENCE
After partner has bid two suits responder may choose to play in the first suit bid despite the fact that he is longer in the second. See PREFERENCE.

FAST ARRIVAL
This principal stresses the manner of reaching the final contract. Quickly would show a weakish hand by the leaper, with no slam interest. Slowly would show good values and possible interest in greater things. For instance, the auction of 1♠ - 2♣ - 2♦ - 4♠ should be a sign off by the 4♠ bidder, but 1♠ - 2♣ - 2♦ - 3♠ would guarantee a spade game and indicate a possible slam.

FEATURE
A potentially useful holding in a suit.

FIELD
All the players entered in an event.

FIELDING A PSYCHE
A psyche is said to be fielded if the partner (before the psyche can legitimately be shown to have been exposed in the subsequent course of events) produces an abnormal and unexpected action which protects his side from damage which might result from the psyche. See PSYCHIC BID.

FIFTH ACE
As the trump King is often as important as an Ace, some conventions treat the King of trumps as the "fifth" Ace. See FIVE ACE BLACKWOOD.

FILM

(British) A conventional defense to an opening pre-emptive three level bid. The acronym stands for **FI**shbein and **L**ower **M**inor. Over an opening 3♦ or 3♥ bid, Fishbein (the next suit up) is a take out request guaranteeing four cards in the bid major, and 4♣ is for take out denying four cards in the Fishbein major. Over an opening 3♣ or 3♠ bid, the lower minor is a take out request. See DEFENSE TO OPENING THREE BID, FISHBEIN, LOWER MINOR.

FINAL BID

The last bid before three consecutive passes end the auction.

FINESSE

An attempt to win a trick with the lower ranking card when leading towards a tenace. For example:

A Q

3 2

If West has the King, this suit will yield two tricks if South leads towards the tenace, playing the Queen unless the King appears. A finesse position arises in a number of different forms but all of them depend on the assumption that a particular card or cards may be held in a certain hand. See CHINESE FINESSE, DEEP FINESSE, DOUBLE FINESSE, FREE FINESSE, OFFSIDE, ONSIDE, REPEATED FINESSE, RUFFING FINESSE.

FIRST IN HAND (FIRST HAND)

The dealer, the first player to have the opportunity to open the bidding.

FISHBEIN

The use of a bid of the next suit (e.g. 3♥ - 3 ♠) after a three level pre-emptive opening as a take out request. Sometimes called "Herbert." See DEFENSE TO OPENING THREE BID, FILM.

Harry Fishbein

FISHBOWL

(British) Method of allowing tournament bridge to be viewed by an audience. The players sit inside a large glass surround, enabling the spectators to watch without disturbing the players.

FIT

1) The combined holding in a suit.

2) The two hands of a partnership are said to fit well if, for instance, one player has only small cards (hence no wasted values) in a side suit in which his partner is void.

FIVE ACE BLACKWOOD

A version of Blackwood in which the King of the agreed trump suit is treated as a fifth Ace. In response to 4NT:

5♣	Shows zero or three Aces.
5♦	Shows one or four Aces.
5♥	Shows two Aces.
5♠	Shows five Aces.

FIVE CARD MAJORS

Some systems require that an opening bid of 1♥ or 1♠ guarantees at least a five card suit.

FIVE CARD SPADES

Some systems require that an opening of 1♠ guarantees five cards, but 1♥ does not.

FIVE CARD STAYMAN
After a 1NT or 2NT opening bid, 2♣ or 3♣ asks partner to bid a five card major. The diamond response denies the holding. If responder has a four card major he now bids it and opener will confirm a 4 - 4 major suit fit if one exists.

FIVE OF A MAJOR OPENING
This conventional opening shows an eleven playing trick hand missing both top trump honors. Responder passes with neither top honor, raises to six with one of the two top honors, and to seven with both top honors.

FIVE SUIT BRIDGE
A game devised in 1937 by Dr. Marculis of Vienna, using a 65 card deck containing 5 suits of 13 cards each. It did not achieve lasting popularity.

FIXED (FIX)
A colloquialism meaning that a pair has received a bad score through no fault of its own.

FLANNERY
A convention invented by William Flannery to deal with the troublesome situation when a player is dealt four spades, five hearts and a minimum opening bid (11-15 HCP). An opening bid of 2♦ describes this hand. The responder bids 2♥ or 2♠ to play, 3♥ or 3♠ invitational, 4♣ or 4♦ as transfers to 4♥ and 4♠, or 2NT to inquire about opener's distribution and strength.

FLAT
Evenly distributed (4-3-3-3). A racontuer might refer to a hand which was distributed 7-2-2-2 as a flat hand. See FLAT HAND, SQUARE HAND.

FLAT BOARD

In duplicate pairs, a hand on which the same result was scored by all the contestants. In teams, a hand on which both sides recorded the same score.

FLAT HAND

A balanced hand, particularly the 4 - 3 - 3 - 3 pattern.

FLINT

A convention invented by Jeremy Flint designed to allow the partnership to play in three of a major after the bidding has been opened with 2NT. The Flint 3♦ response asks opener to rebid 3♥ after which the Flint bidder will either pass or convert to 3♠.

Jeremy Flint

FLITCH

(British) Competition for married couples.

FLOAT

Three passes at the end of the auction, as in 1NT, float.

FLOGGER

(British) Sheet recording the results of previous rubbers.

FOLLOWING SUIT

Each player's first legal obligation, to play a card of the same suit that was led to the trick if possible.

Following Suit

FORCE

1) To make a forcing bid.

2) To make an opponent ruff in order to shorten trumps in one of the hands. It is often used as a defensive maneuver.

FORCED BID

A bid that a player is forced to make, usually because the system that is being played so requires.

FORCING BID

A bid which requires partner to make at least one further bid.

FORCING 1NT

A convention whereby a response of 1NT to an opening of one of a major is forcing for one round. It is frequently used in conjunction with strong (game forcing) two over one responses.

FORCING CLUB SYSTEMS

Any system which uses an opening one club bid as artificial and absolutely forcing. This bid usually indicates 16+ HCP and it demands some response by partner. 1♦ is usually used as the artificial negative response.

FORCING DEFENSE
Often an effective defense is simply to continue "pumping" (forcing declarer to ruff in the long trump hand). This type of defense has the dual benefit of shortening declarer's trump holding and making the declarer break the new suits himself rather than doing this for him.

FORCING PASS
1) A pass which forces partner to bid or double. Often when a player has to make the decision between doubling a sacrifice bid made by an opponent or bidding on himself, he may pass and let his partner make the final decision.

2) Systems utilizing the opening call of "Pass" as a positive bid.

FORCING SEQUENCE
A bidding sequence which by partnership agreement is forcing.

FORCING TO GAME
See GAME FORCING BID.

FORCING TWO BID
The use of an opening two level bid as an unconditional, natural game force.

FORWARD GOING
A description of an encouraging bid.

FOSTER ECHO
A combination count signal and unblocking play against notrump contracts. When a lead is made, if the third hand either cannot top the card led or cannot top the card played from the dummy, the Foster Echo convention requires him to play his second-highest card in the suit. If third hand has three cards in the suit his next play in the suit will be the highest card; if he has four cards in the suit his next play will be his third highest, followed by his highest, then his lowest.

FOULED BOARD

A board in which one or more cards have been interchanged to different pockets. This usually occurs after some post-mortem when the players are not careful about replacing the cards in their correct place. This creates a real headache for the director, who must determine at what precise point in play the board was distorted, and adjust the scores accordingly.

FOUR ACES SYSTEM

A 1930's bidding system used by the Four Aces to win many championships. This system featured weak jump overcalls, psychic bids, 3 card minor suit bids (when the mood struck). The point count structure was A = 3, K = 2, Q = 1, J = 1/2 and 11 1/2 to 13 point opening one notrump bids, using the above guidelines.

FOUR CARD MAJORS

Systems which do not guarantee more than four cards in the suit when a major suit is opened.

FOUR DEAL BRIDGE

See CHICAGO.

FOUR NO TRUMP CONVENTION

Bid with various artificial meanings. See BLACKWOOD, BYZ-ANTINE BLACKWOOD, CULBERTSON 4-5 NT, D.I., FIVE ACE BLACKWOOD, GENERAL PURPOSE CUE BID, RO-MAN BLACKWOOD, ROMAN KEY CARD BLACKWOOD.

FOURTH HIGHEST (FOURTH BEST)

The standard lead from a long suit with no honour sequence.

FOURTH IN HAND

The player who is fourth to call, the player to the dealer's right.

FOURTH SUIT FORCING
After a partnership has bid three suits, it is unlikely that the fourth suit is the best fit. Therefore a bid of the fourth suit can usefully be played as an artificial one round force asking partner to describe his hand further. The bid does not promise any particular holding in the bid suit.

FOXU
A conventional defense to an opening three level pre-emptive bid. FISHBEIN is employed sitting Over the bidder and double (X) sitting Under, as take out requests. See DEFENSE TO OPENING THREE BID.

FRAGMENT BID
An unusual jump or double jump bid showing a fit for partner's suit and a shortage in the fourth suit. See SPLINTER BID.

FREAK (HAND)
A hand or complete deal with an extremely abnormal distribution.

FREE BID
A free bid is one made after an oppponent has intervened, thus releasing the "free bidder" from any obligation to bid.

FREE DOUBLE
At rubber bridge it refers to the double of a game bid (or a partscore contract which if successful would make game whether doubled, undoubled or redoubled). It is not of course "free" but is likely to be less costly than doubling the opposition into game.

FREE FINESSE

Term used to describe a finesse declarer can take without being disadvantaged should it fail. For example:

♥ K J 2

♥ A 4 3

West leads a heart and South finesses the Jack. See FINESSE.

FREE RAISE

Raise of partner's suit in competition which usually does not imply extra strength.

FRIGID

Slang term for a "certain" contract. "Cold" and "Icy" are similar terms.

FRUIT MACHINE SWISS

See SWISS CONVENTION.

FULFILL THE CONTRACT

Taking as many tricks in the play of hand as contracted for in addition to book; for example, nine tricks in a contract of three.

GADGET
A convention or part of a convention.

GAMBIT
The deliberate sacrifice of a trick in order to gain two or more tricks as a result.

GAMBLING 3NT
An opening bid of 3NT to show a long and solid minor, at least A K Q x x x, with no more than an outside Queen.

GAME
1) The 100 points scored below the line in rubber bridge.

2) 100 or more trick points scored on one deal in duplicate bridge.

GAME ALL
In rubber bridge when both sides have previously won a game and are thus both vulnerable. In duplicate or Chicago when the pre-determined vulnerability so indicates.

GAME BID
A bid of just enough tricks to make game: 3NT, four of a major, or five of a minor. In rubber bridge, if the partnership already has points towards game, the bid may be at a level sufficient to convert that partscore into game.

GAME CONTRACT
Any contract which if successful will yield enough tricks to make game.

GAME FORCING BID
A bid which demands that the partnership does not stop short of game.

GAME INVITATION
A bid which does not force the partnership to game but invites partner to bid it with extra values, in the context of his previous bidding.

Game Invitation

GAME TRY
A bid that suggests interest in game and asks partner to reassess his values and make the final decision.

GAME TRY DOUBLE
A double made in a competitive auction, when both sides have bid and supported a suit, as a means of distinguishing between a competitive raise of partner's suit and a game invitation. The double is the game invitation, and the immediate raise is thus purely competitive.

GARBAGE
Slang term for a poor hand.

GARDENER 1NT OVERCALL
An overcall of 1NT to show either a strong no trump (15 - 17 or 16 - 18 points) or a weak hand with a long suit.

GENERAL PURPOSE CUE BID
A bid of 4NT used as a general slam try when a cue bid is not available or convenient.

GERBER

A convention whereby a bid of 4♣ asks about the number of Aces held by partner. In response:

4♦   Shows zero or four Aces.
4♥   Shows one Ace.
4♠   Shows two Aces.
4NT   Shows three Aces.

Subsequently 5♣ enquires about Kings with corresponding responses. See ROLLING GERBER, ROMAN GERBER.

GET A COUNT (OF THE HAND)

To discover the distribution of the unseen hands either as declarer or as defender.

GHESTEM

A system of strong two-suited overcalls devised by Pierre Ghestem of France:

Over 1♣:   2NT   Shows the red suits.
                    2♦   Shows the majors.
                    3♣   Shows the other suits (diamonds and spades).

Over 1♦/1♥/1♠: 2NT   Shows the lowest two unbid suits.
                             3♣   Shows the highest two unbid suits.
                     Cue bid.   Shows the other two suits.

GIN

A certain contract.

GIVE COUNT

To make a distributional signal.

GLADIATOR

A system of responses to a 1NT opener: 2♣ demands 2♦ which responder can pass or convert to 2♥ or 2♠. 2♦ is now the Stayman inquiry (2NT denying a four card major), 2♥ and 2♠ now game forcing with a five card suit. A jump to three of a major is now a slam invitation.

GO DOWN

To make fewer tricks than contracted for.

GO FOR A (TELEPHONE) NUMBER

See NUMBER, GOING FOR A.

GO GAME

To bid a game.

GO IN

A defender in second position who plays the Ace when declarer leads low towards dummy is said to "go in" or "go up" with the Ace.

GOLD POINT(S)

Type of points awarded by ACBL for overall placing in Regional and National events. Section tops also receive gold points. In recent years, some special events have allowed moderate amounts of gold to be won in local clubs (Epson, Royal Viking, etc.)

GOOD

Adjective used to describe a hand in which every card is a winner. e.g. "Dummy is good." "High" is used in the same sense.

GO OFF

To make fewer tricks than contracted for.

Dr. Kalman Apfel, Charles H. Goren and Tobias Stone,
clutching the Spingold Trophy in 1956.

GOREN (POINT COUNT) SYSTEM
See STANDARD AMERICAN.

GOULASH
A method of dealing when the cards are not shuffled after the initial deal and play. Five cards are dealt at once in turn to each player. This is repeated for a second round, before a further three cards are dealt at once to each player. As one might expect, hands dealt this way are often wildly distributional.

GO UP
See GO IN.

GRAND COUP
A trump coup in which winners must be ruffed to shorten declarer's trumps. The name comes from the early days of whist when it was then thought that such a play deserved a high-sounding title. See TRUMP COUP.

GRAND SLAM

To bid a grand slam is to contract to make all thirteen tricks. See BONUS.

GRAND SLAM FORCE

Invented by the Culbertsons and published by his wife Josephine in Bridge World (the convention was often referred to as "Josephine"). A bid of 5NT, not preceded by 4NT, after a trump suit has been agreed asks partner to bid seven holding two of the top three trump honours or, holding less than two, to sign off in six of the trump suit. More sophisticated responses have been devised to give extra information.

GREEK GIFT

A trick offered to the opposition which, if accepted, leads to disaster.

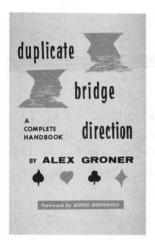

GRONER

"Duplicate Bridge Direction" authored by Alex Groner has been the official director's manual for many years. It features charts on Howell, Mitchell, Swiss Team, Board-a-Match and Individual movements.

GROSVENOR GAMBIT

Originally described (by Frederick Turner in "The Bridge World" in a somewhat tongue-in-cheek manner) as an intentional misplay in a suit that would allow the opposition to pick up an extra trick. Since no intelligent opponent would believe such an irrational play had been made, the normal result is achieved. But the opponents are left swearing under their breath.

$$K\ 8\ 7\ 6\ 5\ 3$$

$$Q\ 10\ 4 \qquad\qquad 9$$

$$A\ J\ 2$$

Declarer leads the ace and West plays the 10. On the lead of the jack West plays the 4. Now, no declarer would ever take the finesse (since West could always have a trick just by playing the 4 first) but when East shows out most declarers tend to become a little irritated. A few years later, however, Kit Woolsey wrote a follow-up article and found some legitimate applications.

GUARD

A card combination which prevents the opposition from immediately running tricks in a suit.

Guard

GUARD SQUEEZE

Squeeze against one opponent in two suits and in a third suit that opponent must keep certain card(s) (the guard) to prevent his partner from being finessed.

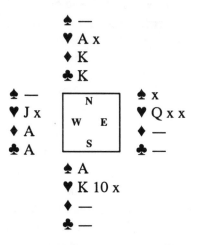

```
                 ♠ —
                 ♥ A x
                 ♦ K
                 ♣ K
   ♠ —          ┌─────────┐      ♠ x
   ♥ J x        │    N    │      ♥ Q x x
   ♦ A          │  W    E │      ♦ —
   ♣ A          │    S    │      ♣ —
                └─────────┘
                 ♠ A
                 ♥ K 10 x
                 ♦ —
                 ♣ —
```

When South leads the ace of spades West must hold the two aces so he is forced to part with a heart. This allows South to make the last 3 tricks by finessing in hearts.

GUIDE CARD

A card used to instruct contestants to which table they should move after the end of each round, either given to each contestant, or placed on each table.

H

HALF TABLE
A table at which only one pair is sitting.

HALF TRICK
An honor holding which can be expected to win a trick half the time such as K x, or the Queen in a holding of A Q (one and a half tricks).

HAMILTON
See CAPPELLETTI OVER NOTRUMP.

HAND
1) The thirteen cards held by a player.
2) The set of four hands.
3) The position at the table, as in "First in hand" (the dealer).

HAND HOG
A player who goes out of his way to play as many hands as possible, often by bidding no-trump quickly.

DON'T BE A BIDDING HOG

ONE SPADE TWO SPADES THREE SPADES FOUR SPADES FIVE SPADES SIX SPADES...

HANDICAPPING
To impose a penalty on the stronger members of the field to allow the weaker players a chance of victory.

HAND PATTERN
The distribution of the cards in a player's hand according to suit.

HAND RECORDS
In an important match, a record of the hands, the bidding, the play and the result, which is kept for future analysis. See CURTAIN CARD.

HARD VALUES
Aces and Kings. By comparison Queens and Jacks are called "soft values."

HARDY PUBLISHING
One of the major bridge publishers, founded by Max Hardy and acquired by Baron Barclay Bridge Supplies in 1991.

HEART
1) The second-ranking suit in bridge.
2) The symbols on this suit's cards.

HELP SUIT GAME TRY
After a major suit opening has been raised to the two-level, opener's minimum level bid of a new suit asks responder to bid game (in the opened major) if he holds help in the new suit. Depending on partnership agreement, various criteria may be used for "help."

HERBERT NEGATIVE
A bid of the next step up (e.g. 2♥- Pass - 2♠) as a negative response to strong two opening bid. Over 2♠ some players use 2NT as the negative response, others use 3♣.

HESITATION
A noticeable break in tempo in either the bidding or play. Some of the most difficult (and emotional) directorial situations arise from hesitations.

HIDDEN ENTRY
An entry that is not readily available, but with some care may be established, usually by unblocking high cards.

A K Q 3

J 10 9 2

Needing four entries to dummy declarer must take care to overtake the J, 10, and 9 with the A, K and Q so that when the suit splits in the expected 3-2 manner, the 3 in dummy will be the fourth entry.

HIGH
See GOOD.

HIGH CARD
    1) An Ace, King, Queen or Jack.
    2) A card that has become established.

HIGH CARD POINTS
(HCPs)
Numerical measure of a hand's playing and defensive strength counting an Ace as four points, a King three, a Queen two and a Jack one and discounting distributional points. See MILTON WORK COUNT.

High Card Points

HIGH-LOW SIGNAL
The play of an unnecessarily high card on the first round of a suit, and a lower card on the second round as a method of signalling. It is also known as an "Echo" or a "Peter."

HIGH REVERSE
A rebid by opener in a lower ranking new suit at the three level after a two over one response, e.g. 1♠ - Pass - 2♦ - Pass - 3♣. It is a bid which is normally played as forcing to game. See LOW REVERSE.

HIPPOGRIFFS
The fictional suit used by the Devil in a famous bridge story, "The Green Suit."

HIT
Colloquialism for double.

HOBSON'S COUP
See MERRIMAC COUP.

HOG
A person who attempts to become the declarer as often as possible. Thus the phrase "To hog the bidding." See HAND HOG.

HOLD
    (1) To have a particular card in hand.
    (2) To lead and win the trick, thus holding the lead.
    (3) To have a non master card win a trick, such as "the Jack held the trick."

HOLDING
Particular cards in a player's hand, as in "A good club holding."

HOLD OFF
See HOLD UP.

HOLD UP (PLAY)
Decline to win a trick, often with the intention of disrupting opponents' communications.

HONEYMOON BRIDGE
A somewhat unlikely term to describe various forms of two-handed bridge.

HONOR(S)
One of the five highest cards in a suit i.e. the Ace, King, Queen, Jack or 10.

Be careful where you play your honors — they are big cards.

HONOR LEAD
The lead of an honor card.

HONORS
In rubber bridge or Chicago bridge, any player holding four or five honor cards in the trump suit or holding all four Aces in a no trump contract may claim for "Honors" and score a bonus. See BONUS.

HONOR STRENGTH
The value of a hand in terms of honor tricks.

HONOR TRICKS

As defined by Culbertson, an honor trick was the basic unit of defensive value. The overall value of a hand was calculated by totalling the number of honor tricks in each suit:

A K	Two honor tricks.
A Q	One and a half honor tricks.
A, K Q or K J 10	One honor trick.
K x or Q J x	Half an honor trick.

In addition "plus values" were deemed to be worth approximately one quarter of an honor trick. Plus values were: Any Queen which was not a singleton, any Jack supported by another honor (but not a doubleton combination nor in a suit holding of A K Q J), any singleton or void (but not more than one).

    Today, the term Quick Trick is used more frequently than Honor Trick.

HOOK

To finesse.

HOUSE PLAYER

A player at a rubber bridge club "employed" by the management to make up tables.

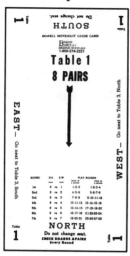

HOWELL (MOVEMENT)

Cyclic pairs movement, usually dictated by movement guide cards, allowing competitive play with as few as two tables. Unlike Mitchell movements pairs change direction at some tables. In a full Howell movement all the pairs will play all the other pairs. See MITCHELL, THREE QUARTER MOVEMENT.

HOYLE, Edmond
First codifier of the rules of Whist. His famous work of 1742, briefly entitled "A Short Treatise on the Game of Whist Containing the Laws of the Game and also Some Rules Whereby a Beginner May, with Due Attention to them, Attain to the playing It Well," became a best-seller.

HUDDLE
A prolonged hesitation.

HUM
(British) With the advent of many weird and wonderful systems and conventions, the Laws have deemed some as "**H**ighly **U**nusual **M**ethods" or HUMs.

ICY
Slang term for describing a certain contract. "Cold" and "Frigid" are similar terms.

IDAK
See WONDER BIDS.

IDIOT COUP
An attempt to make an unwary declarer take a rather foolish finesse.

```
              K Q 8 4
    10 5 3              J 9 5
              A 7 2
```

Declarer cashes the ace and follows with the two. On the second round West plays the 10 and East drops the nine. Declarer may be fooled into thinking West has erred and split from J 10 fourth, returning to hand to try a finesse.

A close relative of the Grosvenor Gambit.

IDLE CARD (BIDS)
A card not required for a specific purpose as distinct from a busy card. The term usually applies to unimportant cards in squeeze positions.

ILLEGAL CALL
Any insuffect bid or any bid or call made out of rotation.

I.M.P.(S)
See INTERNATIONAL MATCH POINTS.

IMPOSSIBLE NEGATIVE
In response to a strong 1♣ opener playing the Precision Club, it is common with a 4-4-4-1 shape and positive values to make the negative response of 1♦ and a forward-going move on the next round. The rebid means that the initial response was an "Impossible Negative."

IMPROPER CALL
Any bid or call made by a player who is under obligation to pass.

INADMISSABLE CALL
Any illegal double or redouble; any bid of more than seven; any call after the auction is closed. One difference between inadmissable and illegal calls is that illegal calls may be accepted by an opponent; inadmissable calls are automatically cancelled.

IMPROPRIETY
A breach of ethical conduct.

IN BACK OF
Term describing the position of a player with respect to his right-hand opponent and therefore being able to play after him. See IN FRONT OF.

IN FRONT OF
Term describing the position of a player with respect to his left-hand opponent and therefore having to play before him. See IN BACK OF.

INCOMPLETE RUBBER
If a game of bridge has to be terminated before the end of a rubber, bonuses are awarded depending on the state of the rubber. For scoring see BONUS.

INCOMPLETE TABLE
A table at which fewer than the necessary four players are sitting, and especially a half table at duplicate.

INDICES
The letter or number in the corner of playing cards, above the suit symbol. Most European cards use double indices; most American cards have a single index.

INDIVIDUAL MOVEMENT
A movement used in an event where individual players score separately, competing with different partners against one another.

INFERENCE
A conclusion drawn about the likely lie of the cards from the previous play and bidding.

INFERENTIAL COUNT
An assessment of the entire distribution of the concealed hands, based on evidence from the bidding and the early play.

INFORMATORY DOUBLE
Old term for take out double. See TAKE OUT DOUBLE.

INSPECTION OF TRICKS
In rubber bridge any player may inspect the previous trick until his side has played to the next trick. In duplicate he may not do so after he has turned his own card over. He may however inspect, but not expose, his own card until a card has been led to the next trick.

INSTANT MATCHPOINTING
A method of scoring hands as if they had been played in a duplicate event by comparing the score obtained with a pre-determined chart.

INSUFFICIENT BID
A bid not legally sufficient, i.e. below the level of the minimum allowable bid. The Laws apply.

INSULT

A bonus of 50 points for making a doubled contract is commonly referred to as "50 for the insult." The same applies to the 100 points awarded for making a redoubled contract. See BONUS.

INSURANCE BID

Sacrifice bid against a high level contract by the opposition despite some expectation of defeating that contract.

INTERFERENCE (BID)

Any overcall or double which denies the opponents an uncontested auction.

INTERFERENCE WITH BLACKWOOD

See DEPO, DOPE / ROPE, DOPI / ROPI, PODI, ROPE, ROPI.

INTERIOR SEQUENCE

A sequence of honor cards (but including the 9) comprising two or more touching cards with one higher non-touching honor. For example, A J 10 9, K J 10, Q 10 9.

INTERMEDIATE CARDS

Tens, nines and eights.

INTERMEDIATE JUMP OVERCALLS

A jump overcall based on a good opening hand with a six card suit.

INTERMEDIATES

Cards which may become winners as the cards that outrank them are played.

INTERMEDIATE TWO BIDS

In days of yore, these were used to indicate a hand just below game-guaranteed values. The responder could pass if he had a terrible hand.

INTERNATIONAL BRIDGE PRESS ASSOCIATION (I.B.P.A.)
The worldwide organization composed of authors and columnists which arranges press coverage of bridge events.

INTERNATIONAL MATCH POINTS (I.M.Ps.)
Used as a method of scoring in teams matches. The aggregate difference between the scores of the opposing teams on each board is converted to International Match Points on a pre-set sliding scale. In certain events a further conversion is made to Victory Points. See VICTORY POINTS.

INTERNATIONAL POPULAR BRIDGE MONTHLY
English bridge magazine published and edited by Tony Sowter.

INTERVENING BID
An overcall.

INVERTED MINOR SUIT RAISES
This convention "inverts" the normal meanings of the single and double raises of a minor suit. Thus 1♦ - Pass - 2♦ is stronger than 1♦ - Pass - 3♦. See DOUBLE RAISE.

INVITATIONAL BID (INVITATION)
A bid that encourages partner to bid on holding any extra values in the context of his previous bidding.

IRON DUKE (Not through the)
A humorous remark made by a player covering an honor or splitting honors. Any comment made at the table is illegal and unethical, however mirthfully intended.

IRREGULARITY
A deviation from the rules or procedures set forth in the Laws or Proprieties of Bridge.

ISOLATING THE MENACE

A method of leaving only one player in the position of guarding a particular suit, thus increasing the chance of executing a successful squeeze. See SQUEEZE, THREAT CARD (MENACE).

J

JACK
The fourth-ranking card in each suit; the knave.

JACOBY TRANSFERS
Invented by Oswald Jacoby, a response of 2♦ (2♥) over an opening 1NT shows at least five cards in hearts (spades). See TRANSFER BIDS.

Oswald Jacoby

JACOBY 2 NT
A convention employed by the responder after partner has opened with one of a major suit. A 2 NT response indicates a forcing raise (usually with four trumps) of unlimited strength without a singleton. Opener now clarifies his holding thusly:

3 of any side suit shows a singleton or void in that suit

4 of any side suit shows another five card suit

3 of the original major shows 16+ points and slam interest

4 of the original suit shows no slam interest and a minimum opener

3 NT shows 14-15 HCP and a balanced hand.

Variations are popular such as showing a singleton at the 3 level and a void at the 4 level.

JETTISON (SQUEEZE)
To discard a high honor (usually Ace or King), often to create an entry for partner or to unblock a suit.

JORDAN
The conventional understanding in which a jump to 2 NT by responder, after the opener's bid is doubled for takeout, shows a limit raise in opener's suit. Also See CAPPELLETTI OVER NOTRUMP.

JOKER
An extra card used in some games though not in bridge.

JOSEPHINE
See GRAND SLAM FORCE. (Named after Josephine Culbertson; see page 52 for her photo.)

JOURNALIST LEADS

A complete system of opening leads as follows:

Against no trumps: Ace from a strong holding (e.g.
                            A K J x or A K 10 x).
                        King from a weaker holding.
                        Queen from Q J x or a weak K Q x
                            holding.
                        Jack from J 10, but no higher honor.
                            10 from an interior sequence (e.g.
                            A J 10 x or K 10 9 x).
                            9 from 10 9 x.
                        Lowest from a suit headed by an honor
                            (but not one of the above honor
                            combinations).
                        Second highest from suits without an
                            honor.

Against a suit contract: Lower of two touching honors.
                        Third and fifth from an honor or non-
                            touching honors.
                        Top of nothing.
See LEADING FROM HONORS.

JUMP BID (JUMP REBID)
Any bid at a level higher than neces-
sary to show the denomination. See
STOP.

Jump Bid

JUMP CUE BIDS
As the name implies, this is a bid in the opponents' suit while
skipping a level of bidding. Examples are Andersen, Denial and
Mandell.

JUMP OVERCALL
A single jump bid made as an overcall.

JUMP PREFERENCE
To return partner to his original suit at the same time making a
jump bid.

JUMP RAISE
A bid which raises partner's suit two levels of bidding.

JUMP SHIFT
A jump in a new suit by the responding hand missing out one
level. The bid is normally forcing to at least game level unless
made by a Passed hand. In the latter case it normally promises a
near opening bid, a fair suit and support for partner's suit.

JUNIOR
In international competition, a player under the age of 25.

JUNK
A worthless hand or suit.

KAMIKAZE NOTRUMP
This system uses an opening bid of one notrump in first or second position to show a balanced hand with 10-13 high card points. The hand must not contain a singleton or void, but it may have a six-card suit or even a seven-card suit. It need not have stoppers in any specified number of suits.

KAPLAN-SHEINWOLD (K-S) SYSTEM
Devised by Edgar Kaplan and Alfred Sheinwold, this system features:
    5 card major suit opening bids
    Opening psychic (lead-directing) bids
    Weak two bids
    Negative doubles
    Forcing 1 NT after major openings
    Limit jump raises
    Weak (12-14 HCP) No Trump opening bids
    Sound minor suit opening bids

KEM CARDS
All-plastic playing cards, first manufactured in 1934 in the U.S.A. Kem cards come in many designs and are very durable, outlasting plastic-coated cards.

KEY CARD BLACKWOOD
See FIVE ACE BLACKWOOD, ROMAN KEY CARD BLACKWOOD.

KIBITZER

An onlooker at the card table. The word is of Yiddish origin and refers to the natural, lively curiosity displayed by the Kiebitz, a native bird (about 32 centimeters long) of central Europe that winters in Africa.

Kibitzer

KICKBACK

The Kickback convention conserves useful space by using a bid other than four notrump as the (key-card) asking bid when the trump suit is other than spades. When trumps have been agreed, the Kickback bid is four of the suit just above the trump suit:

Agreed Trump Suit	Kickback Bid
Clubs	4♦
Diamonds	4♥
Hearts	4♠

KILLED

Removed the entries to a particular hand (Usually the dummy, as in the king of diamonds lead killed the dummy).

KING

The second-ranking card in each suit.

KISS

Acronym for "Keep it simple, stupid."

KISS OF DEATH
A penalty of 200 points at duplicate, usually a disastrous result, almost certainly being worse than any partscore that could be made by the opposition.

KITCHEN BRIDGE
Social bridge played with little emphasis on technique.

KNAVE
The original name for the fourth highest ranking card in a suit. It is now more usually called the Jack in order to avoid confusion with the King when hands are recorded.

KNOCK
> 1) At rubber bridge, an alternative to "Pass."
> 2) See ALERT.

KNOCK OUT
To force an opponent to play a master card (e.g. "To knock out the Ace").

KNOCK OUT TOURNAMENT
Head to head teams of four competition with the losers being eliminated.

KOCK - WERNER REDOUBLE (KOCH-WERNER)
An SOS redouble named after its Swedish inventors. It asks partner to seek a better contract. See SOS REDOUBLE.

ℒ

LANDY
A conventional defence to a 1NT opener whereby 2♣ shows at least 5-4 in the majors, in response to which the only artificial bid is 2♦, asking for the longer major. See DEFENSE TO INT.

Alvin Landy

LATE PAIR
Various duplicate movements make provision for a pair arriving after the start of a session but its admission is at the discretion of the Director.

LATE PLAY
Completion of a board not played during the allotted time.

LAVINTHAL
See McKENNEY.

LAVINTHAL SIGNALS (DISCARDS)
Suit preference signals, originally devised by Hy Lavinthal in 1934, are useful in discarding, leading or following suit.

There are two methods by which suit preference discarding signals may be given; both have been called Lavinthal. The first is similar to the Suit Preference Signals, in which the rank of the card played corresponds with the rank of the suit the defender wants led.

The other method of making suit preference discards, also called Revolving Discards, treats the suits as a complete circle, with clubs ranking above spades. Using this method, the discard of a low card in a suit calls for the lead of the next lower ranking suit; the discard of a high card calls for the lead of the next higher ranking suit. See SUIT PREFERENCE SIGNAL.

LAW OF SYMMETRY
See SYMMETRY OF DISTRIBUTION.

LAW OF TOTAL TRICKS
Theory suggesting that the total number of tricks available to both sides is equal to the sum of the lengths of the two trump fits. It may be used in deciding whether a sacrifice will be profitable and for other close competitive decisions.

LAWS
The "Laws of Duplicate Contract Bridge" or the "Laws of Contract (Rubber) Bridge."

LAWS OF CONTRACT BRIDGE
The international code under which rubber bridge is played. They are promulgated by The Portland Club, The European Bridge League and The American Contract Bridge League.

LAWS OF DUPLICATE CONTRACT BRIDGE
The international code under which duplicate bridge is played. They are promulgated by the World Bridge Federation in association with the same bodies as the Laws of Contract Bridge.

LAYDOWN
Term for a contract that is so certain that declarer could claim after the initial lead.

LEAD
The initial card played to a trick.

LEAD DIRECTING BID
A bid made with the intention of suggesting an initial lead in that suit.

LEAD DIRECTING DOUBLE(S)
A double of a conventional or cue bid to suggest a lead of that suit.

LEADER
The person who is required to play the first card to a trick.

LEADING FROM HONORS
The standard leads from honor combinations are:

> Ace from A K (but King from A K doubleton).
> The higher of two touching honors.
> Top of a doubleton.
> Low (e.g. fourth highest) from other combinations.

Notes:
1) Some players prefer to lead the King from A K.
2) Against a suit contract it is usual not to underlead an Ace.
3) Against a no trump contract the lead of an honor usually guarantees the possession of at least three honor cards unless the lead is from a short suit. From a long suit headed by just two (touching) honors, the standard lead is a low card (e.g. fourth highest). See JOURNALIST LEADS, ROMAN LEADS, STRONG KINGS AND TENS.

LEAD INHIBITING BIDS

A bid of a suit not held in strength, in the hope that the opposition is discouraged from leading the suit.

LEAD OUT OF TURN

A lead from the wrong hand. The Laws apply.

LEAD THROUGH

A player who leads to a trick is said to lead through the player on his left.

LEAD THROUGH STRENGTH

In general, a player sitting in front of dummy and unsure which suit to lead, should lead through dummy's stronger holding, in the hope or knowledge of leading up to partner's honors in the suit. For example (with North as the dummy):

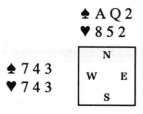

♠ A Q 2
♥ 8 5 2

♠ 7 4 3
♥ 7 4 3

West, on lead with no definitive information to guide him, should lead a spade.

LEAD UP TO WEAKNESS

In general, a player sitting over dummy, and unsure which suit to lead, should lead up to dummy's weakness in the hope or knowledge of leading up to partner's honors in the suit. For example (with North as the dummy):

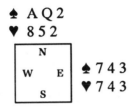

♠ A Q 2
♥ 8 5 2

♠ 7 4 3
♥ 7 4 3

East, on lead with no definitive information to guide him, should lead a heart.

LEAP

A jump bid often used to describe a jump to the probable final contract inviting partner to Pass at his first opportunity.

LEAVE IN

To pass and especially to pass a penalty double by partner.

LEBENSOHL

The bid of 2NT after intervention over partner's 1NT opening to allow responder to distinguish between a strong hand and a competitive hand. Traditionally a direct suit bid at the three level is strong and a bid via 2NT (which requests opener to bid 3♣) is merely competitive.

LEG
Colloquial term for a game in a rubber.

Leg

LEGAL (CALL)
Any bid or call that is not a violation of the Laws. (i.e., is in rotation, is sufficient, is proper and is not inadmissable).

LENGTH
The number of cards held in a particular suit.

LENGTH SIGNALS
See COUNT SIGNALS.

LEVEL
The number of tricks above the book named in the bidding. See BOOK.

LHO
Abbreviation for <u>L</u>eft-<u>H</u>and <u>O</u>pponent.

LIFE MASTER
Original honor given to 10 players in the 1930s based on their achievements at national tournaments. The highest ranking in the American Contract Bridge League, based on masterpoints earned.

LIFT
Term meaning "Raise."

LIGHT
1) To be light means to go down in a contract.

2) To bid light means to bid with values below the acceptable range.

LIGHTNER DOUBLE
A double of a freely bid slam by the player not on lead to the first trick and calling for an unusual lead. The suit called for is normally the first bid side suit of the hand which is about to become the dummy and often shows a void in the suit. See DOUBLE.

LIMIT BID
A bid which defines a player's hand very accurately in terms of both strength and distribution, for example the 1NT opener and the 2♠ bid in the sequence 1♠ - Pass - 2♠.

LIMIT RAISE
A raise of partner's suit to an appropriate level on the assumption that partner has the lower range of values for his bid. It is not forcing.

LIMIT RESPONSE
A response which defines the strength of the responder's hand, e.g. 1♠ - Pass - 3NT.

LINE
1) The horizontal line dividing a rubber bridge score sheet, hence the expressions "Above the line" relating to penalties, overtricks and bonuses, and "Below the line" for tricks bid and made.

2) The plan of play (as in "The best line of play").

3) When (typically) four card suits are bid in ascending order they are said to be bid "up the line."

LITTLE MAJOR
System developed by Jeremy Flint and Terence Reese in the 60's, featuring artificial one bids (clubs shows hearts, diamonds shows spades, spades shows a minor and one heart is strong and forcing).

LITTLE ROMAN CLUB
The Little Roman Club System, also called Arno, is similar to the Roman Club system, especially in its two-level opening bids. All one-level openings, including one notrump, are forcing. The opening bid and responding style is canape.

A forcing one club opening may be made on either of two types of hands. It may show a balanced hand with 12 to 16 points, or a one-suited or two-suited hand worth 17 to 20 points.

LITTLE SLAM
See SMALL SLAM.

LOCK
An unbeatable contract. (i.e., "7 NT was a lock.") Also, any sure thing. See also COLD, FRIGID.

LOCKED (IN OR OUT OF HAND)
To be unable to get the lead in or out of dummy or declarer's hand without loss.

L.O.L.
Abbreviation originally for "Little Old Ladies." Of any age and either sex, they often star in experts' tales of woe after getting a bad result from a seemingly innocuous pair.

LONG CARDS
Cards left in a suit when all other cards in the suit have been played.

LONG HAND
The hand with the greater length in a particular suit, particularly the trump suit.

LONG SUIT
A suit with four or more cards in the same hand.

LOSER
A card which will lose a trick if it is led or played in following suit.

LOSER ON LOSER
To discard one losing card on another. Here is an example where it is good play:

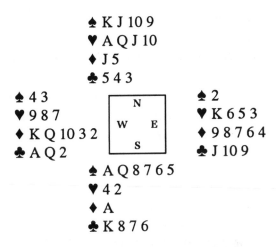

```
            ♠ K J 10 9
            ♥ A Q J 10
            ♦ J 5
            ♣ 5 4 3
♠ 4 3                      ♠ 2
♥ 9 8 7          N          ♥ K 6 5 3
♦ K Q 10 3 2   W   E        ♦ 9 8 7 6 4
♣ A Q 2          S          ♣ J 10 9
            ♠ A Q 8 7 6 5
            ♥ 4 2
            ♦ A
            ♣ K 8 7 6
```

South plays in 4♠ and receives the lead of the diamond King. If East obtains the lead with the King of hearts, there is the danger of three club losers in addition to a heart loser. Therefore, after drawing trumps, declarer should play dummy's Jack of diamonds (West from his lead is presumed to hold the Queen) and discard a losing heart. He can then establish heart tricks by taking a ruffing finesse into the safe hand.

LOSE THE LEAD
The gaining of the lead by an opponent, whether by design, by force or by accident.

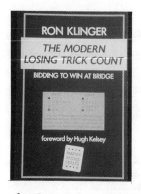

LOSING TRICK COUNT

A method of evaluating the playing strength of a hand based on the number of expected losers. The number of losers is determined as follows: With three or more cards, the number of losers in a suit is equal to the number of missing high honors (the Ace, King and Queen) e.g. A x x counts as two losers, K Q x or K Q x x count as one loser. With a doubleton, the Queen is counted as a small card in the above calculation, and similarly with any singleton, other than the Ace, the suit counts as one loser. The maximum a hand may have is thus twelve, and the most two combined hands could have is twenty- four. So a six loser hand opposite an eight loser hand would have fourteen losers between the two and therefore they should make ten tricks. A simpler approach is to subtract the number of combined losers from eighteen to arrive at the appropriate level to which to bid, hence the four level in the previous example. A player may revalue his LTC in the light of extraordinary trump solidity, or a dearth of high cards. The main advantage of the losing trick count over the Milton Work count is that the losing trick count is more accurate with good trump fits. See MILTON WORK COUNT.

LOVE ALL
Neither side vulnerable.

LOVE SCORE
Neither side vulnerable and, in rubber bridge, no partscore.

LOW CARD
Any card other than an honor card and denoted by an "x" on hand records.

LOWER MINOR

A conventional defence to an opening three bid. Using this convention, a bid of the lower unbid minor (3♦ over 3♣ or 4♣ over anything else) is a take out request. The advantage of this defence is that all other suit overcalls, 3NT and a double can be used in their natural sense. See DEFENSE TO OPENING THREE BID, FILM.

LOW REVERSE

A rebid by opener in a higher ranking new suit at the two level. This bid is normally forcing for one round. For example: 1♣ - Pass - 1♥ - Pass - 2♦. See HIGH REVERSE.

MAGNETIC CARDS
Special cards which are used with a magnetic board, suitable for play at the pool or beach.

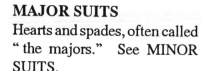

MAJOR SUITS
Hearts and spades, often called "the majors." See MINOR SUITS.

Major Suits

MAJOR TENACE
The holding of the highest and third highest cards in a suit. This combination will always yield one trick and, if the missing card lies in front of the tenace or the opponent with the missing card can be forced to open up the suit, two tricks can be made.
See MINOR TENACE, TENACE.

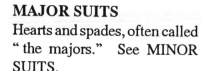

MAKE
1) To shuffle the deck.
2) To make enough tricks for the contract.
3) To win a trick.

MAKE UP A TABLE
For a fourth player to join with three others to play a game of bridge.

MAMA-PAPA BRIDGE
Slang for very simple natural bridge.

MARKED CARD
A card that is known to be in a particular hand.

MARKED FINESSE
A finesse when one opponent is marked with the missing card.

MARMIC SYSTEM
Unusual system used in the past years by various Italians. Passing with strong (16-19 HCP), balanced hands was one of the oddities.

MASTER
A player of some competence. There are, however, a considerable number of different levels of master.

MASTER CARD
The highest outstanding card in a suit.

MASTER HAND
The hand with control of the trump suit.

MASTER PAIRS (MASTERS)
An event, usually by invitation, for players of the highest caliber.

MASTER POINTS

Points issued by the national bridge organizations, and sponsoring organizations which are affiliated to them, for achievement in their competitions. Their accumulation enables the holder to be classified as a certain rank and the organizations regularly publish promotions and rankings.

MATCH

One event of a team game. In board-a-match, one board is a match. In some International competitions, more than two hundred boards may comprise a match. Most of the time, however, a match consists of seven boards in modern Swiss Team play (usually 8 matches are played in an event) and about 32 boards in Knockout events.

MATCH PLAY

Head to head competition. See POINT A BOARD.

MATCHPOINT(S)

In a duplicate pairs event, the result of the conversion of a pair's absolute score on any board to a ranking score. One matchpoint is awarded for every pair beaten and one-half for every pair with the same score. To matchpoint is to do the conversion.

In a team event, to matchpoint is to convert the aggregate difference on any board into I.M.Ps. See FACTORING.

MATHE

An asking bid used by opener to seek a side suit singleton after responder has made a limit raise in a major. Developed by late World Champion and ACBL past President Lew Mathe.

Lew Mathe & Mike Lawrence.

MAXIMAL DOUBLES
Competitive doubles used to invite game when the auction will not allow an alternative game try. For example, you open one heart, LHO bids two diamonds, partner raises to two hearts and RHO bids three diamonds. A double by you would show game interest in hearts, but a three heart bid would be competitive with no game interest.

MAXIMUM
Holding the greatest possible values for one's previous bidding.

McKENNEY
A system of signals / discards showing suit preference. A high signal / discard asks for a lead of the higher of the other two suits (i.e. excluding the suit on which the signal / discard is made and the suit of the signal / discard). Similarly a low signal / discard asks for the lead of the lower of the other two suits. See SUIT PREFENCE SIGNAL.

William McKenney

MECHANICS OF BRIDGE
These deal with definitions, preliminaries, preparation and progression of the game of bridge as defined in the Laws of Duplicate Contract Bridge.

MENACE
See THREAT CARD (MENACE).

MEN'S PAIRS
Bridge event limited to only male participants.

MERRIMAC COUP

The sacrifice of an honor, usually a King, as an entry killing maneuver. For example:

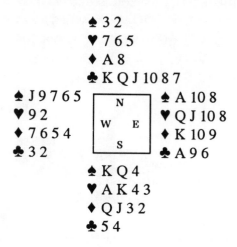

```
              ♠ 3 2
              ♥ 7 6 5
              ♦ A 8
              ♣ K Q J 10 8 7
  ♠ J 9 7 6 5   ┌─────┐   ♠ A 10 8
  ♥ 9 2         │  N  │   ♥ Q J 10 8
  ♦ 7 6 5 4     │W   E│   ♦ K 10 9
  ♣ 3 2         │  S  │   ♣ A 9 6
                └─────┘
              ♠ K Q 4
              ♥ A K 4 3
              ♦ Q J 3 2
              ♣ 5 4
```

West leads a spade against South's 3NT contract. East wins and switches to the King of Diamonds. If South refuses to play dummy's Ace, East plays another diamond. Provided that East ducks the first round of clubs, South cannot come to nine tricks.

The coup is sometimes known as "Hobson's Coup" and the play is likened to Captain Hobson who scuttled his ship, the "Merrimac," to bottle up the Spanish fleet in the Bay of Santiago in 1898.

George Rosenkranz (with glasses) and his teammates in 1975.

MEXICAN TWO DIAMONDS

Designed by George Rosenkranz, this bid shows a balanced hand with 19-21 HCP. It was later amended to show 23-24 balanced points, a strong 3 suited hand or an ACOL two bid in a major suit. It is an important part of the Romex system.

MICHAELS CUE BID

The use of the simple cue bid, i.e. a direct overcall in the suit opened by an opponent (as in the sequence 1♣ - 2♣ or 1♠ - 2♠), to show a two-suited hand. The cue bid of a minor shows the majors and the cue bid of a major shows the other major and a minor suit, after which 2NT is an enquiry as to which minor suit is held. The original convention admitted hands with 5 - 4 shape but the modern style demands at least 5 - 5. See CUE BID.

MIDDLE GAME

The part of the hand, after the first few tricks, in which the declarer develops the plan of the play or prepares for an endplay (in the end game).

MILTON WORK COUNT

The 4-3-2-1 honor point count used by most players. It was invented by Milton Work and was based on the McCampbell count of 1915. See HIGH CARD POINTS, LOSING TRICK COUNT.

MINIMUM

Holding the fewest possible values for one's previous bidding.

MINI-SPLINTERS

In recognition of the fact that distributional values may compensate for the absence of high card strength, many partnerships use shortness-showing bids with less than the high card strength traditionally needed for a game force. These "Mini-Splinters," may be used either to force game or to invite game, and they may be used not only by responder in support of the opening bid, but also by opener in support of responder's suit.

MINI NO TRUMP

An opening 1NT bid showing 10-12 points.

MINOR SUITS

Clubs and diamonds, often called "the minors." See MAJOR SUITS.

Minor Suits

MINOR SUIT STAYMAN
An artificial response to partner's 1 NT opening bid, searching for a minor suit game or slam. Playing 2-way Stayman, two diamonds could initiate such a probe. Or playing a two spade response to 1 NT opener as a minor suit asking bid, partner responds:

1) with a four card minor if he has one.

2) in his better major at the three level with both four card minors.

3) 3 NT with no possible slam interest.

4) 2 NT with slam interest.

MINOR SUIT SWISS
A convention whereby responses of 3♥ and 3♠ (and optionally 3♦ after 1♣) to an opening of one of a minor show good trump support, sound values for at least 3NT and some slam interest. The convention has the advantage that responder can show his support and values without taking the bidding beyond 3NT. The Swiss response may be used either to show a strong holding in the suit bid or to show specific hand types. See SWISS CON-VENTION.

MINOR TENACE
An original holding of the second and fourth highest cards in a suit, i.e. K J. After one or more tricks have been played, the second and fourth highest cards remaining in the suit. See MAJOR TENACE, TENACE.

MIRROR DISTRIBUTION
See DUPLICATION OF DISTRIBUTION.

MISBOARDING
Term used when the hands are replaced in the wrong slots in duplicate play. If this means that the next table is unable to play the board, then the guilty pair or pairs will usually be fined a number of matchpoints.

MISCUT

At rubber bridge, an illegal cut before dealing the hand which has fewer than four cards in either part of the deck.

MISDEAL

A misdeal occurs if a card is faced during the deal or any player receives the incorrect number of cards.

MISERE

A player is said to have followed a misere (slang) line if his play was inferior, especially very inferior. "Butcher" and "Carve" are similar terms.

MISFIT

Description of a situation when both hands of a partnership contain two long suits but no fit.

MISSING CARD

A card not-to-be-found in any of the four hands. Possible locations: Stuck to another card's back, on the floor or in someone's pocketbook. If the card is never found, the hand (and the deck) are thrown out if the game is rubber bridge. In duplicate bridge, the director determines the missing card and replaces it in the proper hand. There are penalties if this happens after the start of the hand.

MISSISSIPPI HEART HAND

An infamous fixed hand dating from early Whist. It appears one side can easily take all 13 tricks, but due to the strange distribution, the opponents can instead obtain a number of defensive tricks.

MITCHELL (MOVEMENT)

A simple pairs movement in which the N-S pairs remain stationary, the E-W pairs move to the next higher table and the boards to the next lower table. If there is an even number of tables then the middle round is a "skip" round, boards moving as normal, E-W pairs moving up two tables. Alternatively, a "relay" movement is used with the first and last tables sharing boards and a relay set of boards between the middle tables. See HOWELL, SCRAMBLED MITCHELL.

MIXED PAIRS

A competition in which each pair includes a man and a woman. See FLITCH.

Mixed Pairs

MONITOR

A person assigned for special duties during high-level team events. He notes the bids made on his side of the screen and then vocally relays these bids to the players and monitor on the other side of the screen. A monitor might also record the time taken by players to call, in case of a slow play controversy or penalty.

A monitor might also be a person designated to observe a pair whose overachievements are highly suspicious. The monitor could spot an illegal signal being flashed.

MONSTER
A very powerful hand.

Monster

MORTON'S FORK COUP
A term used to describe a play when, like the victims of Henry VII's Lord Chancellor, Cardinal Morton, whatever the defender's answer, it is wrong. Cardinal Morton would periodically collect money from merchants and citizens. His reasoning was that if the people lived well, they could afford to pay part to the king. On the other hand, if they spent little money, they could afford to contribute to him. Either way, they were caught on Morton's Fork. Here is an example:

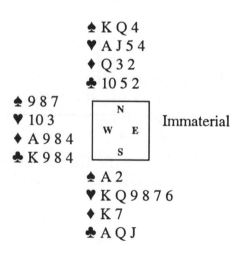

```
                ♠ K Q 4
                ♥ A J 5 4
                ♦ Q 3 2
                ♣ 10 5 2
  ♠ 9 8 7      ┌──────────┐
  ♥ 10 3       │    N     │   Immaterial
  ♦ A 9 8 4    │  W   E   │
  ♣ K 9 8 4    │    S     │
                └──────────┘
                ♠ A 2
                ♥ K Q 9 8 7 6
                ♦ K 7
                ♣ A Q J
```

Playing in a contract of 6♥, South receives a trump lead and potentially may lose a diamond and a club. However, if he plays a small diamond from hand towards dummy's Q 3 2, West has no recourse. If he rises with the Ace, then dummy's Queen will be established for a second club discard (the spade suit taking care of one losing club). If West ducks, declarer is able to discard the King from his hand on a spade and just loses one club.

MOVE

The change of seats by certain players in a duplicate pairs or teams event at the end of each round.

MOVEMENT

A schedule determining where players go at the end of each round. See HOWELL, MITCHELL.

MOVEMENT CARDS

Cards placed on each table in a dupli-cate event directing players to their next table at the end of each round.

MOYSIAN FIT

A 4 - 3 trump suit is said to be a Moysian fit. The term is named after Alfonse Moyse Jr., whose bidding style often resulted in the partnership playing in a 4 - 3 fit.

MUD

Standing for Middle-Up-Down, this is a method of leading from a three card suit (with no honor holding in the suit) by leading the middle card and on the next play of the suit following with the highest card. Partner is therefore able to identify that the suit is not a doubleton.

MULTI

See MULTICOLORED TWO DIAMOND OPENER.

MULTICOLORED TWO DIAMOND OPENER

A conventional 2♦ opener used to show two or three distinctly different types of hand, including at least one weak and one strong type. The most popular version of the convention shows either a weak two bid in a major, or a strong two bid in a minor or a strong balanced hand. Other strong options are a minor two-suited hand and an unspecified three-suited hand (4 - 4 - 4 - 1 or 5 - 4 - 4 - 0). It is popular outside the United States, but seldom seen in American competition.

1932 Nationals in New York City

1964 Nationals in Toronto

NAMYATS
Using standard methods, preemptive openings of four of a major suit may be made on a wide variety of hands. To distinguish the strong major preempts from the weak ones, some partnerships use an opening bid of four clubs to transfer to four hearts, and an opening bid of four diamonds to transfer to four spades. As most frequently used, the openings of four clubs and four diamonds (Namyats) show stronger hands than the direct openings of four hearts and four spades. Namyats is Stayman spelled backwards.

NATIONALS (NAC)
The North American Championships, sponsored by the ACBL and held three times annually during the Spring, Summer and Fall.

NATURAL (CALL)
A suit bid which guarantees some holding in the suit bid, or a no trump bid suggesting the hand is playable in no trumps.

NEAPOLITAN SYSTEM
This highly effective system was designed by Eugenio Chiaradia and played by many of the Italian bridge stars during their reign as International Champions from 1956-1969. This basic system, revised by Benito Garozzo in 1965, is now the Blue Team Club system. This system features:
    The Big Club, artificial and forcing
    Step responses to the one club opening
    Weak two bids in the majors
    A three-suited two diamond opening bid (17-24 HCP's)
    Canapé style.

NEGATIVE DOUBLE

A double after partner has opened the bidding and right-hand opponent intervenes with a suit call, to show values and usually four cards in an unbid major. It is for take out, not penalties. It is also called a Sputnik double, both making their appearance in 1957. See DOUBLE.

NEGATIVE FREE BID

Used by responder to show a hand not strong enough for a forcing bid after an opponent's overcall. Partner opens one diamond, RHO overcalls one spade and you hold: ♠764 ♥KQJ975 ♦64 ♣Q2. If you and your partner have agreed to play negative free bids, you may bid two hearts (non-forcing) here. If you had a better hand, you would have to double (negative) first and then bid hearts.

NEGATIVE INFERENCE

To infer the lie of the cards by considering why an opponent did not choose an alternative line of play.

NEGATIVE RESPONSE

A response denying values, often after a strong artificial opening. See DENIAL BID, HERBERT NEGATIVE.

NET SCORE

The difference between the plus and minus points on a rubber bridge scoresheet or the total IMPs (International Match Points) differential in a duplicate Swiss team game or Knockout match.

NEUTRAL CARD

A card which when played conveys no information other than simply the fact of its existence in that hand as opposed to, for instance, a signal.

NEUTRAL LEAD
See PASSIVE LEAD.

NEW MINOR FORCING
If the opener has started the auction by bidding one club and has rebid one notrump, and the partnership is using a two club rebid by responder as Delayed Stayman, the responder can no longer retreat from notrump into his partner's first suit. To preserve this escape route, some partnerships elect to "check back" by having the responder bid the unbid minor suit over the opener's notrump rebid. Their forcing auction would thus be

Opener	Responder
1♣	1♥
1 NT	2♦

NEW SOUTH WALES SYSTEM
Bidding system developed and used in Australia featuring:
   Five card openings in diamonds, hearts and spades
   Strong 1 NT opening
   Forcing one club opening which is used for a number of different types of hands.

NO BID
Term signifying "Pass." Traditional in Britain. See PASS.

NO CALL
An outdated term meaning "Pass."

NON-FORCING
A bid which does not demand a response from partner.

NON-VULNERABLE (NOT VULNERABLE)
The condition of a side that has not yet won a game. See RED, VULNERABLE, WHITE.

NORTH

One of the positions at the bridge table. In duplicate North has the responsibility for scoring the hand and overseeing the boards at the table.

NO TRUMP

Highest ranking denomination at bridge.

NO TRUMP DISTRIBUTION

A balanced hand; one which contains no void or singleton; usually 4-3-3-3, 4-4-3-2, or 5-3-3-2.

NO TRUMP FOR TAKE OUT

A defense to weak three openings whereby an overcall of 3NT is used as a take out request allowing all other calls to be natural, including a penalty double.

NO TRUMP OVERCALL

A bid of no trump after an opponent has opened the auction.

NOTTINGHAM CLUB

A simple English 1♣ system popular in the Nottingham area. The system is based on an artificial 1♣ opening (16 - 21 points) and five card majors.

Novice

NOVICE
Any new or inexperienced player. In ACBL rankings, someone with less than 20 master-points.

NOVICE GAME
A club or tournament competition limited to novices.

NUISANCE BID
A bid aiming to disrupt the opposition's auction.

Going for a Number.

NUMBER, GOING FOR A (TELEPHONE)
Being set a large number of points. Unlike a sacrifice which is frequently a winning situation, it is usually a very poor result.

OBLIGATORY FALSECARD
Falsecard that will lead to a certain loss if not played.

OBLIGATORY FINESSE
The play of a small card on the second round of a suit in the hope that a particular opponent will have to play the master card. For example:

```
              K 4 3 2
   A 8                    J 10 9
              Q 7 6 5
```

The only way to avoid two losers in the suit is for South, declarer, to play a small card towards dummy and, after winning the King, play small from both hands. If the East-West hands were reversed, it would be necessary to play initially from the North hand towards South's Q 7 6 5.

ODD-EVEN DISCARDS (SIGNALS)
A system of discards in which the face value (odd / even) of the discard is used to signal count, attitude or suit preference.

ODDS
Probability in favor of something occurring compared to the chance it will not happen.

ODD TRICK
Each trick won by declarer in excess of the book. "One odd" is one trick in excess (i.e. declarer's seventh trick). See BOOK.

OFFENDER
A player who commits an infraction of the laws.

OFFENSE
An infraction of the laws.

OFFICIAL SCORE
Final compilation of each pair's matchpoints; not ultimately official until after the correction period.

OFFICIAL SYSTEM
System developed by 12 leading authorities in 1931 in opposition to Ely Culbertson.

OFFSIDE
When a finesse is wrong the missing card is said to be offside. See FINESSE, ONSIDE.

OGUST REBIDS
The Ogust convention systematizes the opener's rebids over the forcing response of two notrump. Choosing one of four steps, the opener describes the strength of his hand and the quality of his suit:

    3♣ = weak hand, weak suit
    3♦ = good hand, weak suit
    3♥ = weak hand, good suit
    3♠ = good hand, good suit

Some partnerships have agreed to reverse the meanings of the three diamond and three heart bids.

OLYMPIAD
See WORLD CHAMPIONSHIPS.

ONE BID
A bid at the one level.

ONE CLUB SYSTEMS
Systems which employ an artificial 1♣ opening bid.

ONE NO TRUMP OPENING

A very effective and descriptive opening bid, usually guaranteeing a clearly defined and limited HCP range, with balanced distribution (5-3-3-2, 4-3-3-3 or 4-4-3-2) and stoppers in three suits. Although most players use a 15-17 or a 16-18 HCP range, various systems offer much variety in the point ranges. 10-12, 12-14, 13-15, 14-16, 15-18, 17-20 and even 8-10 are possible ranges.

ONE-ODD

The "odd" tricks are those taken by the declarer's side above 6. So one-odd would be seven tricks taken by declarer's side.

ONE OVER ONE RESPONSE

A sequence such as 1♣ - 1♥, where responder bids at the one level.

ONE SUITER

An unbalanced hand with one long suit and no other suit of more than three cards.

ONSIDE

If a finesse works the missing card is said to be onside. See FINESSE, OFFSIDE.

OPEN

1) To make the first bid in the auction, as in "open the bidding."

2) Teams or pairs competition where no restriction applies to the contestants (sex, age, master point ranking, etc.).

OPENER'S REBID

The second, hopefully descriptive, bid made by the opening bidder, clarifying his holding. Some rebids are quite definitive:

1♥ - Pass - 1 NT - Pass - 2♥ should promise 6 hearts and a minimum (13-15).

1♥ - Pass - 1 NT - Pass - 3♥ should promise 6 hearts and 16-18 points.

1♦ - Pass - 1♠ - Pass - 1 NT should be a balanced minimum (13-14) if your opening notrump range is 15-17.

1♦ - Pass - 1♠ - Pass - 2 NT should be a balanced 18-19 point hand.

1♣ - Pass - 1♥ - Pass - 2♥ should show 13-15 and heart support (probably 4).

1♣ - Pass - 1♥ - Pass - 3♥ should show 16-18 with four card heart support.

OPEN HAND

Dummy.

OPENING BID

The first call of the auction other than pass.

Opening leads are not an exact science,
but there are rules to follow.

OPENING LEAD(S)

The initial lead to the first trick, before the dummy is seen.

OPEN PAIRS
Competition open to anyone, irrespective of age, master point ranking or sex. In many tournaments, where entry to the main event is restricted (a Mixed Pairs event, for example), it is customary for there to be an "Open Pairs" at the same time.

OPEN ROOM
Room where spectators are allowed in a teams of four competition.

OPEN UP A SUIT
Initiate play in that suit whether as declarer or defender.

OPEN UP (THE BIDDING)
Start the auction with a call other than a pass.

OPPONENTS (OPPOSITION)
Often referred to as either "The Bad Guys" or LHO and RHO. These players are your enemy (for the moment).

OPPONENT'S OR OPPONENTS' SUIT
The suit the enemy has bid during the auction or the suit they chose to lead against your contract.

OPTIONAL DOUBLE
A double suggesting all round strength and inviting partner to choose between bidding on or defending. Many players wrongly describe their defence to weak three bids as an optional double, when more accurately they should describe it as a take out double. See DEFENSE TO OPENING THREE BID.

OPTIONS

In playing a hand — Refer to the choices or chances available to declarer. The better declarers like to take lines of play which preserve their options:

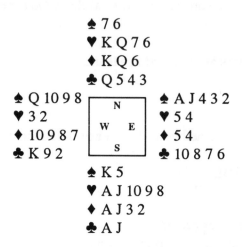

```
              ♠ 7 6
              ♥ K Q 7 6
              ♦ K Q 6
              ♣ Q 5 4 3
♠ Q 10 9 8                    ♠ A J 4 3 2
♥ 3 2          N              ♥ 5 4
♦ 10 9 8 7   W   E            ♦ 5 4
♣ K 9 2          S            ♣ 10 8 7 6
              ♠ K 5
              ♥ A J 10 9 8
              ♦ A J 3 2
              ♣ A J
```

West leads the ten of diamonds versus your 6♥ contract. At first sight it appears you have two possibilities of making the hand. The ace of spades might be in East's hand or the club finesse might work. You can preserve your options by taking these plays in the proper order. After pulling two rounds of trump you lead out four rounds of diamonds, discarding a spade from the dummy. You then get back to dummy with a trump and lead a spade towards your king. If RHO ducks, you play the king. If this should lose to the ace, you can still regain entry to dummy and take the club finesse.

Regarding the opponents' infractions of the rules — The choices given to a player on the non-offending side. For instance, for an opening lead out of turn infraction, the declarer has at least 5 options from which to choose.

ORANGE CLUB SYSTEM
A system originated by James Jacoby and Bobby Wolff. A Big Club system, similar in many ways to the Blue Team Club.

ORIGINAL BID
The first bid made in an auction by a player.

ORIGINAL HOLDING
The cards dealt to a player before any play has taken place.

OUR HAND
Phrase used by a player who thinks his side can make the highest positive score.

OUT
1) Devoid of a suit

2) In Chicago or rubber bridge — Refers to the player sitting on the sidelines while four others play.

OUT-OF-THE-BLUE CUE BID
See ADVANCE CUE BID.

OUT ON A LIMB
Phrase used to describe a dangerous action such as bidding no trumps with no stop in an enemy suit.

Out on a Limb

OVER
Term describing a player's hand with respect to his right-hand opponent, e.g. "Sitting over."

OVERBID
1) Old term for an overcall.
2) A call for which adequate values are not held.

OVERBIDDER
A person who overbids.

OVERBOARD
To be at too high a level.

OVERCALL
1) The first bid by a member of the side that did not open the bidding.
2) To make such a bid.

OVERRUFF
To ruff with a higher trump a trick already ruffed. "Overtrump" is similarly used.

OVERTAKE
To play a higher card from one hand when already winning a trick. Often used when a hand is devoid of entries and the suit is blocked.

OVERTRICK
A trick in excess of the number contracted for. Overtricks do not count towards game and, in rubber bridge, are scored above the line.

OVERTRUMP
See OVERRUFF.

PACK
The deck of 52 playing cards.

PAIR
A partnership of two bridge players.

PAIRS (TOURNAMENT)
An event in which players compete as pairs.

PAJAMA GAME
Duplicate session with numerous tops and bottoms.

PALOOKA
A very poor bridge player.

PAR CONTEST
A contest where marks are awarded based on a player's technique rather than the result, usually with pre-set hands of a technically difficult nature.

PAR (CONTRACT)
The result on a board if both sides have bid and played to the optimum result.

PAR HAND
A hand forming part of a par contest.

PARTIAL
See PARTSCORE.

PARTIAL DESIGNATION
An incomplete request for a card to be played from dummy. If the suit alone is named, the lowest card in the suit must be played. If the rank of the card alone is named, the card must, if there is ambiguity, be taken from the last suit led.

PARTIAL ELIMINATION
A play by which a declarer only partially eliminates the suits which a defender may safely lead when he is thrown in. Whether the defender will have to lead to declarer's advantage depends on distributional factors.

PARTNER
One of the two members of a partnership.

PARTNERSHIP
Two players working as a unit. Bridge is played by two competing partnerships. Partners sit opposite each other. Trust and cooperation between partners are important features of the game.

Partnership

PARTNERSHIP UNDERSTANDING
An agreement between members of a partnership regarding conventions in bidding and play allowing for more efficient communication. Such agreements, whether explicit or implicit, must be fully and freely available to opponents.

PARTSCORE
A trick score of less than 100 points. It is also known as a "partial."

PARTSCORE, BIDDING TO THE
Bidding affected by the presence of a partscore.

PARTSCORE BONUS
See BONUS.

PARTY BRIDGE
These are private bridge games consisting of two or more tables. A pair can have assigned matchups, the losers of a rubber at a table can move down a table while the winners move up a table, or some other arrangement is used. Usually 4 deal (Chicago) bridge is played.

PASS
Call by which a player indicates that he does not wish, or is not allowed by the Laws, to enter the bidding at his turn to bid. See NO BID.

PASSED HAND
A hand which has already passed (and therefore if its holder subsequently makes a bid, that bid is limited in value by his previous pass).

PASSIVE LEAD (PASSIVE DEFENSE)
A lead made more in an attempt to avoid conceding a trick than to establish one.
See ATTACKING LEAD.

PASS OUT (PASSED OUT)

1) A hand is said to be passed out if all four players pass without any player having bid.

At rubber bridge, the deal passes to the next player, at Chicago the same player must redeal, and at duplicate bridge the hands are replaced in the board as if played and the score recorded as no score to either side.

2) To make the third consecutive pass after the bidding has been opened.

PASS OUT OF TURN

A "Pass" by a player when it is not his turn to call. The Laws apply.

PASS OUT SEAT

A player is said to be in the pass out seat if the auction would end if he passed.

PATTERN

See HAND PATTERN.

PENALTY

1) A score arising from the failure of a contract.

2) The sanction imposed by the Laws, or by the Tournament Director, for an irregularity or an infraction.

PENALTY CARD

A card that is wrongly played or exposed may become a penalty card. At duplicate bridge, some penalty cards are designated minor penalty cards, others major penalty cards. At rubber bridge, there is no such distinction. The Laws apply.

PENALTY DOUBLE

A double made in the belief that the opposing contract will not make. It is also known as a "Business double." See DOUBLE.

Penalty Double (although ethical players always double in the same tone of voice).

PENALTY PASS

To pass a non-penalty double thus effectively converting it to a penalty double.

PERCENTAGE PLAY

The line of play most likely to succeed based on mathematical probabilities.

PERCENTAGES

The actual chances (out of 100) that an event will happen. A finesse, for example, is a 50% proposition. Fifty times out of every one hundred times, the finesse will succeed. It's very helpful to a bridge player to know exact percentages, but it isn't absolutely vital. A player doesn't need to know that the odds of four cards splitting 2-2 are about 40% and 3-1 about 50%. It is important for the player to realize that the four cards are more likely to split unevenly and that he shouldn't rely on the 2-2 split.

PERMUTATION

Mathematical term describing all possible arrangements of a set of objects and, in bridge, the possible disposition of the cards.

PERSONAL SCORE CARD
Card used by a player to record his score on each hand. See CONVENTION CARD.

Personal Score Card

PETER
To play an unnecessarily high card in a suit on the first round followed by a lower card on the second. Sometimes called a "high-low signal" or an "echo."

PHANTOM PAIR
If the number of pairs at a duplicate event is not even, there will be a table with only one pair (a half table). In consequence on every round one pair will be due to play the "phantom" pair and will instead spend that round sitting out.

PHANTOM SACRIFICE (PHANTOM SAVE)
A sacrifice bid when the contract against which one is sacrificing could not be made.
See SACRIFICE.

PHONEY CLUB
(British) A rudimentary system based on a strong no trump and five card suit openings in diamonds, hearts and spades, with a (possibly) phoney club being the first move on other hands. "Fishing Club," "Short Club" and "Utility Club" are similar systems.

PIANOLA
A hand of such ease that it "plays itself."

PICK UP
To win a certain number of tricks, or to capture a particular card (e.g. "To play a small spade to hand picking up the Queen").

Pick Up Slip

PIN

```
                A 10 9 8 7
        K 6 5                 J
                Q 4 3 2
```

The lead of the Queen towards the Ace brings in five tricks when, as here, the Jack is singleton and on the right. It is therefore, "pinned" by the Queen.

PINPOINT ASTRO
A modification of the Astro convention that identifies most suit combinations precisely with one bid. The overcalls and the suits shown are as follows:

2♣ = hearts and clubs
2♦ = hearts and diamonds
2♥ = hearts and spades
2♠ = spades and a minor suit

PIP
A design on the front of the playing card showing the card's rank by the number of pips, and the suit by the shape of the pip. Various pips are used in different countries. Hearts, cloves, acorns, leaves etc.

PITCH
To discard.

PIVOT TEAMS
A teams contest whereby members of each team change partnerships so that by the end of the contest every member of each team has played a proportion of the boards with every other member of the team as a partner.

PLACING THE CARDS
The diagnosis of the hand from clues arising from the bidding or play.

PLAFOND
French game which formed the basis of contract bridge. Harold S. Vanderbilt, who more or less invented contract bridge, used the Plafond ("ceiling") scoring method in contract bridge in the form of "games." The popularity of Plafond and closely related games soon waned after the invention of contract bridge.

PLAIN SUIT
Any suit other than trumps. See SIDE SUIT.

PLAN OF (THE) PLAY (PLANNING THE PLAY)
The mental process by which declarer works out the best line of play.

PLASTIC CARDS
Usually used to refer to all-plastic cards (such as Kems) rather than plastic-coated cards. Plastic cards last longer and are much easier to clean, but they still sell far fewer than other cards, because of the relatively high cost.

PLAY
    1) The play follows the auction.
    2) Used to describe an action in the play, e.g. "The key play is to ruff a diamond."

PLAYED CARD
A defender plays a card by placing it face up on the table in front of him. If a defender places a card in such a position that the other defender can see the front of the card, it is deemed to have been played. Declarer plays a card in a similar manner and any card placed face up, on or near the surface of the table, by declarer is deemed to have been played. Declarer plays dummy's cards by either naming them (the correct procedure in duplicate bridge) or physically handling them (in rubber bridge).

PLAYER
One of the four people who participate in a game of bridge.

PLAYER NUMBER
Each person who joins the ACBL is given a seven digit identifying number. Should the player become a Life Master, the first digit is replaced by a letter.

PLAYING A KNOWN CARD
If a player has the choice between cards, it is sometimes better to play that which he is known to hold. For example:

```
              A J 4
   Q 10 8              5 3 2
              K 9 7 6
```

South, declarer, plays a small card and successfully finesses the Jack. When the Ace is played West should drop the Queen (the card he is known to hold) presenting South with a choice of plays, finessing East for the 10 or playing for the even break. If West follows with the 10 on the second round declarer will inevitably play for the break.

PLAYING CARDS
The set of fifty-two cards with which the game of bridge is played. The pack consists of four suits, clubs, diamonds, hearts and spades (ascending rank order) each containing thirteen trick cards: Ace, King, Queen, Jack, 10, 9, 8, 7, 6, 5, 4, 3, 2 (descending rank order), the rank indicated by a pictorial representation and/ or the number of pips, the suit indicated by the shape of the pip.

PLAYING TO THE SCORE
To allow one's decisions regarding bidding or play to be influenced by the score. Typically to underbid at rubber bridge with a partscore.

PLAYING TRICK
A card which can reasonably be expected to win a trick given a normal distribution of the cards and ignoring the possibility of losing tricks to ruffs; e.g. A K Q x x x is six playing tricks and A K Q x x x x is seven.

PLAY OUT OF TURN
The play of a card when it is not one's turn to play. The Laws apply.

PLOB
PLOB is a convention used by responder after an opening bid of one club or one diamond, a response of one heart or one spade, and a rebid by opener of one notrump, to obtain additional information. The acronym PLOB was adopted by adherents of this convention, after one commentator characterized the convention as a "petty little" "odious" bid.

PLUS VALUES
See HONOR TRICKS.

POCKET
Part of a duplicate wallet or board used to hold the cards.

Duplicate Wallets.

PODI
Method of coping with intervention after partner's Blackwood bid. **P**ass shows zero (**O**) Aces. **D**ouble shows one (**I**) Ace and the lowest bid two etc.

POINT A BOARD
One scoring method of determining a winner in a teams of four match. Each board is taken individually, one point is scored for a win and half a point for a tie. In Britain it is more common to award two points for a win and one for a tie. See BOARD-A-MATCH.

POINT COUNT
A method of hand valuation by points, the most popular of which is the Milton Work count: four for an Ace, three for a King, two for a Queen, one for a Jack. See DISTRIBUTIONAL POINT COUNT.

POINTED SUITS
Diamonds and Spades, so called because of the shape of their symbols. Clubs and hearts are similarly called "Rounded Suits."

POINTS
    1) Measure of hand value. See DISTRIBUTIONAL POINT COUNT, HIGH CARD POINTS, POINT COUNT.
    2) See MATCHPOINT(S).
    3) See MASTER POINTS.
    4) See INTERNATIONAL MATCH POINTS (I.M.Ps).
    5) See POINT A BOARD.

POOL
The stake put up by the contestants to be split among the winners. The ACBL sets limits (quite low, as the ACBL frowns on gambling) on the amount of money a pool may contain.

POPULAR BRIDGE
An American bi-monthly magazine which was founded in 1967 and ceased publication in the '80s.

PORTLAND CLUB, THE (OF LONDON)
First body to codify the Laws of Bridge (1895). Originally The Stratford Club, it was reorganized to remove an unpleasant member. It is still an important authority in the world of international bridge and holds the copyright to the Laws in many parts of the world.

PORTLAND RULES
Rules laid down by The Portland Club which included banning the use of any conventional bids in the club's cardrooms.

POSITION
1) The cardinal compass point (N - S - E - W) of a player.

2) A player's position in relation to the dealer (first hand is the dealer, second hand is on the dealer's left etc.), or in relation to another player; to sit over / behind (to be the left-hand opponent) or under / in front of (to be the right-hand opponent).

POSITIONAL FACTOR
The value of a particular holding may change as the auction develops, thus indicating the likely disposition of the other relevant cards. For instance a holding of K x in a suit is more valuable if the suit has been bid by the right-hand opponent rather than by the left-hand opponent. Thus the positional factor affects its value.

POSITIVE RESPONSE
A constructive response guaranteeing some conventionally agreed minimum strength.

POSITIVE SLAM DOUBLES

When the opponents have reached a slam after an auction in which the defending partnership has bid and raised a suit, the partnership may find it advantageous to use Positive Slam doubles in order to determine whether it should sacrifice or should instead try to set the slam. Unlike Negative Slam doubles, they are made with hands containing one or more defensive tricks, rather than with hands containing no defensive tricks.

POSTING THE SCORE

To place the recapitulation sheet where it is clearly visible to the competitors.

POST MORTEM

Term applied to that period following the completion of a hand when it is analysed by the players.

Post Mortem

POUND (POUNDED)

Defeat the opponents handily.

POWERHOUSE

A hand of tremendous trick taking ability.

PRECISION (CLUB)

A bidding system that originated in Taiwan and was developed by C.C. Wei in the 1960s. It achieved world attention when the team from Nationalist China finished second in both the 1969 and 1970 World Championships. The system is based on an artificial 1♣ (16+ points) opening and five card majors.

PRE-DEALING

The dealing of the hands in advance of the competition in which they are to be played. See SIMULTANEOUS PAIRS.

PREEMPTIVE BID

A weak high level bid based upon the playing strength contained in a long suit, with few outside values. The bid is purely obstructive in nature and can make opposing bidding extremely difficult. See RULE OF TWO AND THREE.

PREEMPTIVE JUMP OVERCALL

Bidding a long suit with a generally weak hand, skipping one or more levels over the opponent's last call.

PREEMPTIVE RAISE

A raise based on distributional rather than high card values in an attempt to pre-empt the opponents, rather than necessarily reach a makeable contract (e.g. 1♠ - Pass - 4♠).

PREFERENCE

To prefer partner's first bid suit after being offered a choice. For example in the sequence: 1♥ - Pass - 2♣ - Pass - 2♦ - Pass - 2♥, responder has given preference for hearts over diamonds, although since opener's first suit will invariably be at least as long as his second, responder would show "preference" for opener's first suit if his two holdings were of equal length. Responder would "prefer" the second suit by passing or raising. See FALSE PREFERENCE.

PREMATURE LEAD
When one defender leads to the next trick before his partner has played to the current trick.

PREMATURE PLAY
When a defender plays out of turn before his partner has played.

PREMIUM
At rubber bridge, any points scored above the line. See ABOVE THE LINE, BELOW THE LINE, RUBBER BRIDGE.

Contract Bridge Score Sheet
— INDIVIDUAL SCORES —

PLAYERS						
1st Rubber						
2nd Rubber						
3rd Rubber						
TOTALS						
WE	THEY	WE	THEY	WE	THEY

PREPARED BID
An opening bid in a low-ranking suit (often, a suit of only three cards), made so that a higher-ranking suit will provide an easy, space-saving rebid.

PREPARED CLUB
An opening bid of 1♣ made on a balanced hand with possibly only a three card (or even two card) club suit to prepare for a no trump rebid.

PREPARED HANDS
See PAR CONTEST, SIMULTANEOUS PAIRS.

PREPARED MINOR SUITS
An opening bid of 1♣ or 1♦ made on a balanced hand with possibly only a three card suit to prepare for a no trump rebid.

PREPAREDNESS, THE PRINCIPLE OF
The principle whereby one selects an opening bid so that one always has a sound rebid over any possible response.

PRESSURE BID
A bid made at a high level due to the presence of interference bidding. For example, after 1♠ - 3♣, responder may have to bid 3♠ with 7-8 points and some spade support, less than that required for an uncontested 3♠ bid. Such a bid is said to be a pressure bid.

PRIMARY SUPPORT
Four card support for an opening bid of one. See SECONDARY SUPPORT.

PRIMARY VALUES
Aces and kings.

PRINCIPLE OF RESTRICTED CHOICE
See RESTRICTED CHOICE.

PRIVATE SCORE
See CONVENTION CARD.

PROBABILITY
The relative frequency of the occurence of an event; the ratio of the number of cases favorable to the event to the total number of cases.

PROBABLE TRICK
A card which has a reasonable chance of winning a trick, according to the auction. If your RHO bid spades and you hold the king in that suit (protected by a small card), your Kx would be a probable trick.

PROFESSIONAL

A bridge professional is a person who makes his living from the game of bridge, though not necessarily as a player.

PROGRESSION

    1) The movement of pairs in a duplicate pairs event.
    2) The movement of the boards in a duplicate event.
    3) The movement of the players in progressive bridge.

PROGRESSIVE BRIDGE

A form of social bridge with several tables in play. The winners on a round move up a table while the losers stay put (or vice versa).

PROGRESSIVE SQUEEZE

This is a repeating triple squeeze against one opponent which ultimately gains two tricks. In both of these hands you, as South, lead out your ace of clubs. One opponent must protect all the other suits. Watch him squirm.

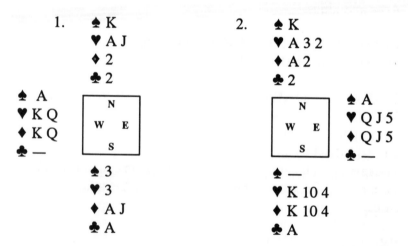

PROMOTION

The play of one card to promote another to winning status. See TRUMP PROMOTION.

PROPRIETIES
The rules of proper conduct, ethics and etiquette.

PROTECT
    1) To possess small cards with an honor in a suit e.g. a "protected" King.

    2) To bid after two successive passes in order that partner may have the opportunity to bid again. See BALANCING.

    3) To have a positional stopper. For example:

```
              K 5 4
Q J 10 2               A 9 7 3
              8 6
```

North's holding protects him from a lead by East, but not by West.

PROTECTION
See BALANCING.

PROTEST (PROTEST PERIOD)
The period of time, usually thirty minutes, after the score has been posted within which one may require an error in the score to be corrected or may register an appeal against a Tournament Director's ruling. See SCORING CORRECTIONS.

PROVEN FINESSE
A finesse that is guaranteed to win because of a prior disclosure. For instance, when South leads the jack from his hand and plays the 3 from dummy after West plays low, East shows out. The subsequent finesse against West is now proven.

```
              A Q 6 3
K 7 4                    void
              J 10 9 8 5 2
```

PSEUDO SQUEEZE

A defender may be presented with the problem of choosing one of two discards, both of which would cost a trick, in which case he has been genuinely squeezed. If only one discard concedes a trick but he has no way of knowing which is the correct card to throw, he can claim to have fallen foul of a pseudo squeeze. Normally he will have enough information to deduce which is the fatal discard but given skilful declarer play his dilemma may be acute. See SQUEEZE.

PSYCHIC BID

A bid which deliberately and substantially misstates the strength and/or distribution of a hand. See CONTROLLED PSYCHES, FIELDING A PSYCHE.

PUDDING RAISE

(British) A balanced raise based on high card strength alone.

PULLING TRUMP

Leading your trump suit until all of the opponents' trumps are drawn.

PUMP

Colloquialism for forcing declarer to ruff. See FORCING DEFENSE.

PUNCH

To force a player to shorten his trumps by ruffing. See SHORTEN.

PUNISH

Double for penalties.

PUPPET STAYMAN

A version of Stayman for five card and four card suits following an opening bid of one or two no trumps. After 1NT- Pass - 2♣- Pass - 2♦ (denying a five card major), responder bids the major in which he does not hold four cards. See STAYMAN CONVENTION.

PUSH

1) To make an unconstructive raise in a competitive situation. The tactic is usually employed in the hope that the opponents will overbid.

2) A board in a teams match with zero swing.

QUACK
Signifies the queen or the jack when the cards are interchangable in the bidding or play.

QUALIFYING
In many duplicate events which consist of more than one session, a pair must qualify for the final session by scoring in the top half or top third of the field during the first session. This limits the number of entries for the final session.

QUANTITATIVE 4NT
The use of 4NT, usually as a direct raise of no trumps, to request partner to pass or bid 6NT depending on whether he is minimum or maximum in the context of the previous bidding.

QUANTITATIVE 5NT
The use of 5NT, usually as a direct raise of no trumps, to request partner to bid 6NT or 7NT depending on whether he is minimum or maximum in the context of the previous bidding.

QUANTITATIVE SLAM (GAME) TRY
Bid that asks partner to pass or bid on, based strictly on the number of high-card values he holds.

QUEEN
The third-highest card in each suit.

QUEEN OVER JACK
An assumption, made in rubber bridge, that the Queen lies over the Jack more often than simple probabilities suggest. It is derived from the theory that in a previous hand the Queen may have covered the Jack and that, after the trick was gathered, the two had not been separated by the shuffle.

QUESTIONS, ANY
In American duplicate games, usually asked by opening leader of his partner before turning over the led card.

QUICK TRICK(S)
See HONOR TRICKS.

QUITTED TRICK
In duplicate bridge a trick is quitted when all four players have turned their cards over. In rubber bridge a trick is quitted when the four cards making up the trick are gathered by the winning side. In duplicate a quitted trick may not be inspected although a player may look at, but not expose, his own card until a card is led to the next trick. In rubber a player may inspect the previous trick until his side has played to the next trick.

RABBI'S RULE
Humorously stated it says, "When the king is singleton, play the ace!" This was attributed to New Yorker Milton Shattner, known as the "Rabbi."

RABBIT
An inexperienced player.

Rabbit

RACK
Apparatus to hold cards for handicapped players.

RAGS
A poor holding, e.g. "two rags," a low doubleton.

RAISE
To increase the level of the contract in partner's last mentioned denomination.

RANK
    1) The relative value of the cards.
    2) The status achieved in a ranking system.
    3) The rank of the suits as used to distinguish between the major suits (spades and hearts) and the minor suits (diamonds and clubs).

RANKING SYSTEMS

National bridge organizations have ranking systems to measure a player's ability. See MASTER POINTS.

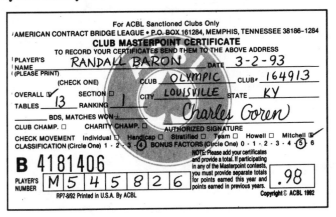

RATING POINT CERTIFICATE

A small piece of paper authorized and printed by the ACBL. This certificate is issued by an ACBL affiliated club to reward a player for placing within a section and earning master points during club competition. The number of fractional points issued depends on:

1) How high the player places
2) The number of tables in the section
3) The type of club (open or restricted)
4) The bonus points to which the club is entitled.

Players amass these rating point certificates and send them in to the ACBL, where they are recorded.

REBID

1) Bid the same suit a second time.
2) Any bid chosen at one's second turn.

REBIDDABLE SUIT

A suit of at least five cards in many instances. Sometimes a strong five card suit or longer holding is needed to rebid the suit, depending on the auction.

RECAPITULATION SHEET (RECAP SHEET)

Sheet on which the results of each board, the totals for each pair and the final placings are posted after a duplicate event. See PROTEST PERIOD.

Recap Sheet

RECTIFYING THE COUNT

The concession of a trick or tricks in preparation for a squeeze in order that, when the squeeze card is played, one opponent must discard while possessing only busy cards. For example:

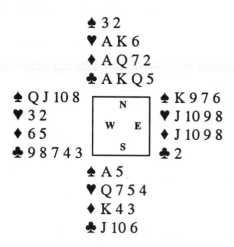

```
              ♠ 3 2
              ♥ A K 6
              ♦ A Q 7 2
              ♣ A K Q 5
♠ Q J 10 8                  ♠ K 9 7 6
♥ 3 2           N           ♥ J 10 9 8
♦ 6 5        W     E        ♦ J 10 9 8
♣ 9 8 7 4 3     S           ♣ 2
              ♠ A 5
              ♥ Q 7 5 4
              ♦ K 4 3
              ♣ J 10 6
```

South, playing in 6NT receives the lead of the Queen of spades. Clearly the contract will be simple if either red suit divides 3 - 3. South can give himself an extra chance by allowing the first trick to hold, thus rectifying the count and ensuring the success of the slam whenever either red suit splits 3 - 3 or when either opponent holds four cards in each red suit. Without rectifying the count, East can never be squeezed. See SQUEEZE.

RED

Being vulnerable at duplicate bridge; at rubber bridge, having won one game in the rubber. See NON-VULNERABLE, VULNERABLE, WHITE.

RED DOT

A marking placed on a convention card signifying that non-standard leads are being employed.

REDEAL

A second or subsequent deal following an irregularity during the original deal.

REDOUBLE

A call which doubles the value of tricks bid and made, the penalty for undertricks and the bonuses for overtricks of a doubled contract. It also leads to an additional bonus ("for the insult") of 100 points if the contract is made. See SOS REDOUBLE.

RED POINTS

These are masterpoints earned in regionally and nationally-rated events by winning the section or placing overall in an event. Various color (red, silver and gold) points are required for Life Mastership.

RE-ENTRY

A second entry.

REFUSE (TO WIN A TRICK)

See DUCK.

REGIONAL TOURNAMENT
Throughout the U.S. there are 25 districts included in the ACBL realm. Each district is allowed to hold at least two regionals annually where players may compete and attempt to win master-points. These are the most important ACBL tournaments, other than the NACs (North American Championships). In the ABA, regionals are local tournaments and sectionals are the larger ones, the opposite of the ACBL's terminology.

RELAY
A bid, usually the cheapest bid, which does not convey any information but simply marks time while partner describes his hand. It is common in artificial systems.

RELAY SYSTEM
A bidding system which employs relays so that one member of the partnership describes his hand accurately and the other decides the final contract.

RELAY TABLE
Table used for boards not in play, particularly during a Howell movement or a relay Mitchell. See HOWELL, MITCHELL.

REMOVE (A DOUBLE)
To bid again after partner has made a penalty double, signifying an unwillingness to defend the contract.

RENEGE
Old fashioned term for revoke.

REOPENING DOUBLE
A double, intended basically for take out, used by the player in the pass out seat to keep the auction alive. The call is often used by the opener as an effective way of competing after partner has passed over an opponent's intervention, especially if nega-tive doubles are part of the agreed system. See BALANCING.

REOPEN THE BIDDING

A call made by a player who has initially passed and is sitting in the position that, were he to pass, the bidding would end. He may be acting in a balancing role. See BALANCING.

REPEATED FINESSE

To finesse more than once in the same suit against the same opponent. See DOUBLE FINESSE, FINESSE.

REPECHAGE

A form of competition whereby competitors, knocked out in the qualifying stages of the main event, have a second opportunity to qualify for the final of the main event by winning a secondary event.

REPLAY DUPLICATE

A form of duplicate whereby two pairs play the same boards from both positions, popular in the 1920s.

RESCUE (BID)

To take out into what is hoped to be a safer contract.

RESERVE

To have an alternative line of play available, e.g. "To keep the heart finesse in reserve."

RESERVE ONE'S RIGHTS

To warn opponents, in advance, that adjudication from the Director may be sought if damage is thought to have been caused by an irregularity. It is not in any way an accusation that opponents have behaved improperly.

RESPOND (RESPONSE)
To reply, with a bid, to a call made by partner which opens the bidding.

Response

RESPONDER
Opening bidder's partner.

RESPONDER'S REBID
The second bid made by the responder, designed to limit and further describe his holding. When a partnership starts the auction, 1♣ - Pass - 1♥, the only information known about the responder's hand is that he has four or more hearts and 6 or more points. In Standard American, if the opener then bids 1 NT limiting his hand to 12-14 HCP, responder must now make a suggestion as to the final contract. A 2 NT rebid by the responder is invitational in notrump, showing a balanced 11-12 HCP. 3 NT is a closeout (13-17 HCP, balanced). Two spades is forcing. Three hearts is invitational (10-11 points and 6 hearts). Four hearts is a closeout with 6+ hearts and 12+ points.

RESPONDER'S REVERSE
A non-jump rebid by responder in a new suit, higher ranking than his original suit and at the two level or above. For example: 1♣ - Pass - 1♥ - Pass - 2♣ - Pass - 2♠.

RESPONSE
See RESPOND.

RESPONSIVE DOUBLE
After an opening bid of one of a suit, a take out double from partner and a (probably pre-emptive) raise from third hand, a double used conventionally to show sufficient values to compete, but with no suitable bid, is called a responsive double. See DOUBLE.

RESTRICTED CHOICE
The Principle of Restricted Choice is a mathematical principle based on the assumption that, with two cards of equal value, a player will play either of them randomly. For example:

K 10 9 8 7 6

A 3 2

South, declarer, plays the Ace and East (on his right) plays the Queen. Given that with Queen - Jack doubleton, East will play the Jack half the time and play the Queen half the time, East is twice as likely to hold the singleton Queen as he is the Queen - Jack doubleton.

RESULTS MERCHANT
A player whose analysis (in the post mortem) of a hand is based on his knowledge of the disposition of the full 52 cards of the hand rather than the more limited information (e.g. the 13 cards on view during the auction) on which a particular decision had to be made.

RETAIN THE LEAD
To keep the lead by playing a card known to be a winner.

REVALUATION
The mental adjustment to the value of one's hand in the light of the previous bidding. For example a holding of K x is more likely to be useful if it is held in a suit bid by one's right-hand opponent rather than by one's left-hand opponent.

REVERSE

A non-jump rebid in a new suit by opener above the level of two of his original suit. See HIGH REVERSE, LOW REVERSE.

REVERSE SIGNALS / DISCARDS

A method of signalling / discarding whereby a low card is encouraging and a high card is discouraging. This reverses the standard high-low signals / discards. The chief advantage is that, with a doubleton, a player does not need to use what may be an important card, which he cannot afford, to encourage.

REVERSING THE DUMMY

See DUMMY REVERSAL.

REVIEWING THE BIDDING

A player may, at his turn to call, request a review of the auction. At duplicate such a review must be given by an opponent and must include every call including alerts and stop warnings.

REVOKE

To fail to follow suit when able to do so. A revoke becomes established when either member of the offending side plays to the next trick. The Laws apply.

REVOLVING DISCARDS

A system of discards whereby the rank of the discard signals a suggested lead. Against no trump contracts, a discard of a high card asks for the lead of the suit ranking immediately above the suit of the discard (clubs above spades) and similarly for a low ranking discard (spades before clubs). For example:

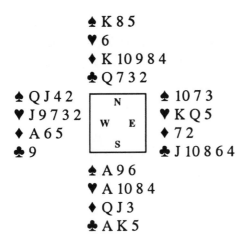

```
                  ♠ K 8 5
                  ♥ 6
                  ♦ K 10 9 8 4
                  ♣ Q 7 3 2
  ♠ Q J 4 2                      ♠ 10 7 3
  ♥ J 9 7 3 2        N           ♥ K Q 5
  ♦ A 6 5        W      E        ♦ 7 2
  ♣ 9                            ♣ J 10 8 6 4
                     S
                  ♠ A 9 6
                  ♥ A 10 8 4
                  ♦ Q J 3
                  ♣ A K 5
```

South, playing in 3NT, receives the lead of the 3 of hearts. East plays the Queen, taken by South's Ace. When South plays diamonds, West holds up his Ace until the third round to allow his partner the chance to signal. Playing revolving discards, on the third round of diamonds the 3 of spades or the Jack of clubs will ask for a heart continuation. See SUIT PREFERENCE SIGNAL.

REWIND
Redouble.

RHO
Abbreviation for **R**ight-**H**and **O**pponent.

RHYTHM
To bid or play in rhythm is to bid or play at an even speed. See TEMPO.

RIDE

To take a finesse by letting a card run round, e.g. : " Let the Queen ride."

A 7 5

Q J 10 3 2

A finesse against the King may be taken by leading the Queen and letting it ride if the King is not forthcoming.

RIFFLE SHUFFLE

An effective form of shuffling by allowing two portions of a pack to become interwoven in a fairly random manner. A perfect riffle shuffle (two portions perfectly interwoven) is thus not a true shuffle at all since a second identical shuffle restores the pack to its original form.

RIGHTS

Privileges to each player under the Laws of bridge. When an irregularity occurs, the director should be summoned to the table in order to protect the rights of all players.

RIPO

A convention initiated after partner's Blackwood 4 NT call is doubled. RIPO is a mnemonic tool, meaning **Redouble = 1** ace, **Pass = 0** aces.

RIPSTRA

A defence to an opening 1NT bid whereby a 2♣ overcall shows both majors with longer clubs than diamonds and a 2♦ overcall shows both majors with longer diamonds than clubs. See DEFENSE TO 1 NT.

ROCK CRUSHER
A hand of tremendous trick taking ability.

Rock Crusher

ROLLING BLACKWOOD
A convention whereby after the response to 4NT, a relay in the cheapest non-trump suit subsequently asks for Kings. It is also called Sliding Blackwood. See BLACKWOOD.

ROLLING GERBER
A convention whereby after the response to 4♣, a relay in the cheapest non-trump suit subsequently asks for Kings. It is also called Sliding Gerber. See GERBER.

ROMAN ASKING BIDS
A method of establishing the suitability of the two hands for slam purposes. In certain situations, when a trump suit has been agreed, a bid of a new suit asks partner to describe his holding on the following scale:

1st step	No control.
2nd step	King or singleton.
3rd step	Ace or void.
4th step	Ace-King or Ace-Queen.

ROMAN BLACKWOOD

A version of Blackwood originally used in the Roman system. After 4NT, the responses are:

5♣   Shows zero or three Aces.
5♦   Shows one or four Aces.

The responses of 5♥, 5♠ and 5NT show two Aces, either of the same color, the same rank or the two other Aces. The original school of thought was:

5♥   Shows two Aces of the same color.
5♠   Shows two Aces neither of which are the same rank nor the same color.
5NT Shows two Aces of the same rank.

Some players prefer the CRO principle, i.e. 5♥ same Color, 5♠ same Rank, 5NT the two Other. A player can then ask for Kings in a similar way. See BLACKWOOD.

ROMAN DISCARDS (SIGNALS)

Odd-even signals, sometimes called Roman signals, are a method of encouraging or discouraging that depends on whether the number of the card played is odd or even, rather than on whether it is high, middle or low. A defender plays an odd numbered card to encourage, or an even numbered card to discourage. In addition, when an even card is played, the size of the card tends to suggest which of the other suits the defender prefers. Roman discards are generally used only on the first discard during a hand. This is the first opportunity when each defender is void in a suit and has a chance to give partner vital information.

ROMAN GERBER

A version of Gerber modelled on the same lines as Roman Blackwood. See GERBER, ROMAN BLACKWOOD.

ROMAN JUMP OVERCALL

A system of two-suited jump overcalls whereby immediate jump suit overcalls show intermediate two suiters, when the lower ranking of two touching suits (excluding the opener's suit) is bid, whilst a 2NT overcall shows a strong unspecified two suiter. See TWO-SUITED OVERCALLS.

Roman Key Card Blackwood

ROMAN KEY CARD BLACKWOOD

In response to 4NT, some players consider the King of trumps as important as an Ace, and thus include it as one in their response to Blackwood. In response to 4NT:

5♣	Shows 0 or 3 Aces.
5♦	Shows 1 or 4 Aces.
5♥	Shows 2 or 5 Aces and denies the trump Queen.
5♠	Shows 2 or 5 Aces and the trump Queen.

After a 5♣ or 5♦ response the 4NT bidder may bid the cheapest non-trump suit to ask about the trump Queen. The responder returns to the trump suit at the minimum level without it, and jumps in the trump suit or cue bids a second round control with it. See BLACKWOOD.

ROMAN LEADS

A system of leads against suit contracts whereby the lower of two touching honors is led. They are sometimes called "Rusinow leads." See LEADING FROM HONORS.

ROMAN SYSTEM (ROMAN CLUB)
System devised by Walter Avarelli and Giorgio Belladonna and used by them as members of the Italian Blue Team. The system is based on an artificial 1♣ opening (either balanced 12 - 16 points or 17+ points) and canape. See CANAPÉ.

ROMAN TWO DIAMOND CONVENTION
A convention whereby a 2♦ opening shows a strong three-suited hand with, typically, 17-20 high card points.

ROMEX SYSTEM
Bidding system devised by Dr. George Rosenkranz of Mexico. The system features a strong two club opening, 1 NT opening to show 21-22 HCP balanced or any unbalanced hand just shy of a two club opening, and a two diamond opening to show a balanced hand with 19-20 HCP.

ROMEX TRIAL BIDS
A method of allowing a player to make both long suit and short suit trial bids, by employing relays after a single raise of a major suit.

RONF
Stands for "Raise Only Non Force." Commonly played in conjunction with Weak Two Bids.

ROPE
After a 4NT enquiry is doubled, Redouble shows an Odd number of Aces, Pass an Even number.

ROPI
After a 4NT enquiry is doubled, Redouble shows zero (O) Aces, Pass one (I), the cheapest bid two, and so on.

ROSENKRANZ DOUBLE
A device used to allow the partner of a player who has overcalled to specify whether his raise of the overcall is made with or without a high honor in overcaller's suit. Overcaller's possession of this information may assist in the defense if the opening side buys the contract.

ROTATION
The sequence and order in which the bidding and play occur at the table.

ROTH-STONE SYSTEM
Developed originally by Al Roth and Tobias Stone in the 1950's and since modified. It features:
> Sound, opening bids in first and second seat
> 5 card major openings
> Forcing 1 NT response
> Constructive raises in the majors
> Weak jump shifts
> Two club opening forcing to game
> Weak two bids

ROUND
The period of time in a duplicate event a pair spend playing against the same opposition.

ROUND OFF ˙
To round off the net score at the end of a rubber to the nearest hundred, with most players rounding fifties down.

ROUND ROBIN
A form of contest in which each competing group (team, pair or individual) plays against every other competing group.

ROUNDED SUITS
Clubs and hearts, so named because of the shape of their symbols. Spades and diamonds are similarly called "Pointed Suits."

ROVER
An additional pair in a Mitchell movement which displaces a different North - South pair each round.

RUBBER
The best of three games in rubber bridge. It is thought that the term "rubber" is derived from the game of bowls.

Rubber Bridge Scoring.

RUBBER BRIDGE
The form of contract bridge in which the objective is to make two games before your opponents and thereby win the rubber. A game can be achieved by scoring 100 points "below the line" either on one deal or by accumulating partscores to reach that total. See ABOVE THE LINE, BELOW THE LINE.

RUBBER DUPLICATE
A teams of four event in which boards are played in a fixed order in both rooms until a rubber is reached in one room.

RUBENSOHL
Uses a combination of Rubens-type Advances and a variation of the Lebensohl convention. It enables either responder or the partner of a player who has overcalled or doubles to compete effectively with both weak and constructive hands.

RUFF
To play a trump on the lead of a side suit in which you are now void.

RUFF AND DISCARD (RUFF AND SLUFF)
To discard a loser from one hand while ruffing in the other.

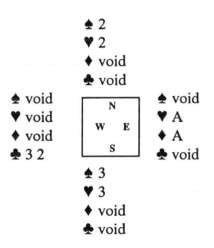

South is declarer and spades are trumps. If any hand other than West is on lead, then a heart must be lost. But with West on lead and obliged to lead a club, South can ruff in dummy and discard a heart from hand. Equally, he could choose to discard a heart from dummy and ruff in his own hand.

RUFFING FINESSE

The lead of one of a sequence of high cards towards a void. If the card is not covered it is allowed to run, if it is covered it can then be ruffed to establish winners. For example:

$$K \; Q \; J \; 10$$
$$9 \; 8 \; 7 \; 6 \; 2 \qquad\qquad A \; 5 \; 4 \; 3$$
$$\text{void}$$

South, declarer, leads the King of a side suit from dummy. If East plays his Ace it is ruffed, thus establishing the Q J 10 as winners. If East plays low South discards a loser. See FINESSE.

RUFFING TRICK

A trick won by a ruff.

RULE OF ELEVEN

A simple mathematical formula which states that if the fourth highest card of a suit is led from one hand then the number of cards capable of beating it in the other three hands is equal to eleven minus the pip value of the card led. For example:

$$K \; 5 \; 2$$
$$7 \; \text{(led)} \qquad\qquad A \; J \; 9 \; 6 \; 3$$

If East judges that the 7 is a fourth highest lead, he can use the rule of eleven to deduce that South has no card higher than the 7. He may play low at trick one to leave West on lead to play a second round of the suit through dummy's King at trick two.

RULE OF TWO AND THREE

The doctrine, in preemptive bidding, that one should not risk going down more than two tricks, if vulnerable, and three tricks if not vulnerable. See PREEMPTIVE BID.

RULING
A decision based upon the Laws of the game, made by a Tournament Director or by an Appeals Committee.

RUN
A suit is said to run if it can be cashed, card after card, without losing the lead.

RUN OUT OF TRUMPS
To have used all the trumps originally dealt to the player or partnership, either because the opponents have pulled trumps or forced him/them to ruff.

RUSINOW LEADS
See ROMAN LEADS.

SAC
A sacrifice (or save).

SACRIFICE (BID)
A bid made in the full expectation that the contract will be defeated, but in the hope that the points lost will be fewer than those that the opponents would have scored had they been left to play in their own contract. See PHANTOM SACRIFICE.

SAFETY LEVEL
The level a partnership is prepared to go to in order to buy the contract.

SAFETY PLAY
A way of handling a suit combination to give the greatest chance of the required number of tricks in the suit at the expense of abandoning the possibility of gaining extra tricks.

SANCTION
Consent given by an organization such as the ACBL or ABA to conduct a bridge tournament or operate a club.

SANDWICH
A bid made in fourth position after both opponents have already had a chance to bid.

SAVE
Used in the same sense as "Sacrifice." See SACRIFICE.

SCHENKEN CLUB

Developed by Howard Schenken. The Schenken system is based on a forcing one club opening bid, with natural responses showing that the responder has high card strength. The one club opening normally shows 17 or more high card points, and may be made on three types of hands. A 1NT opening shows 16-18 HCP. After a 1♣ opening, 1♦ is negative showing less than 7 points; 2♣ is artificial and semi-positive with 7-8 points.

SCISSORS COUP

A play used, as the name implies, to cut communications between the opposing hands, usually to destroy an enemy entry needed to give partner a ruff. For example:

Scissors Coup

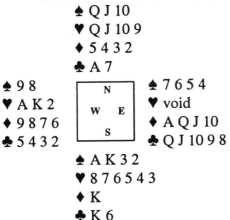

```
              ♠ Q J 10
              ♥ Q J 10 9
              ♦ 5 4 3 2
              ♣ A 7
   ♠ 9 8                     ♠ 7 6 5 4
   ♥ A K 2        N          ♥ void
   ♦ 9 8 7 6    W   E        ♦ A Q J 10
   ♣ 5 4 3 2      S          ♣ Q J 10 9 8
              ♠ A K 3 2
              ♥ 8 7 6 5 4 3
              ♦ K
              ♣ K 6
```

South plays in 4♥. West leads the 9 of spades. At trick two South must play his King of diamonds to snip communications between the opposing hands to stop the ruff in spades. See COUP WITHOUT A NAME.

SCORE (SCORING)
1) The written result of a contract.

2) To obtain a good result on a board, e.g. "We scored on board thirteen."

SCORE CARD
A card for keeping a record and used to score in a teams event, or a personal record in a pairs or individual event. See CONVENTION CARD.

SCORE SHEET
See RECAPITULATION SHEET.

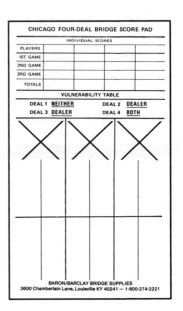

SCORESLIP
1) In rubber bridge or Chicago, printed paper or pad to record the score.

2) In duplicate, the traveller that accompanies the board.
See TRAVELLER OR TRAVELLING SCORESLIP.

SCORING ACROSS THE FIELD
System of scoring against all pairs playing in the same direction instead of scoring each section separately.

SCORING CORRECTIONS
An error in computing or tabulating the agreed score, whether made by a player or a scorer, may be corrected within a timescale set by the sponsoring organization. If no time is set then the period for correction is thirty minutes after the official score has been posted. See PROTEST PERIOD.

SCRAMBLED MITCHELL
A method of producing a single winner from a Mitchell event by arrow switching, on certain rounds, the compass points of the pairs. On such rounds the East - West pairs (and the boards) move normally, but they then play the North - South cards and vice versa. Generally, the final one or two rounds are arrow switched in a scrambled movement. See MITCHELL.

SCRAMBLING
In the play, taking unusual risks and making deceptive plays; anything to try and take tricks that are not readily available.

In the bidding, an attempt to find a more playable (less costly) contract, usually after a low level contract has been doubled for penalty.

SCRATCH
At duplicate bridge, to place in your section or in the overall standings.

Howard Weinstein of the American team communicating with his English opponent on the other side of the screen during the 1993 Maccabiah Games in Israel.

SCREEN

In major championships a large screen is placed diagonally across the table preventing each player from being able to see his partner and one of his opponents. A small slit in the screen allows a tray to slide from one side of the table to the other. The auction is conducted, using bidding boxes, by placing the bids on this tray and repeatedly sliding it from one side of the table to the other. During the cardplay a flap is raised to allow just enough visibility for all players to see the dummy and the cards as they are played. The purpose of screens is to prevent players conveying information to their partners through their mannerisms.

SCREEN-MATE

When screens are in use, he is the opponent seated on one's own side of the screen.

SCRIP

ACBL Award Certificates issued as prizes. May be used at face value for most products or services associated with the ACBL.

SEAT

Each of the four players' positions is designated by a compass direction (North, East, South and West).

Also, there is a numerical designation of bidding turn; the dealer is in first seat and the player to his right is fourth seat.

SECONDARY SUPPORT

A useful holding in a suit bid by partner, often a three card suit as distinct from four card (primary) support. See PRIMARY SUPPORT.

SECONDARY VALUES

Queens and jacks.

SECOND-HAND

1. The next player to have a chance to bid after the dealer.
2. The player who plays immediately after a trick is led to.

SECOND HAND LOW

A favorite maxim of whist play that, following the lead of a small card, the second hand to play to the trick should play the lowest card of the suit led.

SECOND NEGATIVE (HERBERT)

In response to a strong artificial two club opening bid, some partnerships attempt to have the responder distinguish between hands that are weak and hands that are even worse. To achieve this, the responder first makes the negative two diamond response; then over the opener's rebid, he employs this convention by bidding the cheapest suit over the rebid. Some partnerships use the cheaper minor rather than the cheapest suit as the second negative.

SECTION

If a competition field is split into separate groups, each group is called a section.

SECTION MARKERS
Signs at tournaments showing where each group of tables is located.

SECTIONAL TOURNAMENT
In the ACBL, a tournament operated at the Unit level. In the ABA, the most important tournaments after the Nationals, similar in significance to an ACBL Regional.

SEED (ING)
In order to ensure a relatively balanced field within a section, directors assign certain seating positions to the more accomplished players. For example, tables 3, 9 and 14 might be reserved for the better pairs (seeds), both North-South and East-West. In Knockout Team events, the higher the number of masterpoints (averaged per person for 5 or 6 person teams), the higher the seeding the team receives. In the first round of the KO matches, the #1 seed opposes the #64 seed (in a 64 team field), #2 plays #63, etc.

SEMI-BALANCED (HAND)
Hands with 5 - 4 - 2 - 2 or 6 - 3 - 2 - 2 shape.

SEMI-PSYCHIC
A bid which deliberately, but not substantially, misstates the strength and / or distribution of a hand.

SEMI-SOLID SUIT
A suit likely to lose only one trick, even assuming a slightly unfavorable break.

SEND IT BACK
A slang term for redouble. See REDOUBLE.

SENIOR TOURNAMENT
One in which the only eligible participants are 55 years of age or older.

SEQUENCE
Cards in consecutive rank order, for example K, Q, J.

SEQUENCE DISCARDS
The discard of an honor guarantees the honor immediately below it and denies the honor immediately above it.

SESSION
A continuous period of play.

SET
1) To defeat a contract.

2) To set up a suit is to establish it.

3) Set of duplicate boards or wallets. There are usually 32 boards in a set.

4) A pre-arranged rubber bridge match played between two fixed partnerships.

SET A GAME
When the defense accumulates enough tricks to defeat a game contract.

SET GAME

At rubber bridge, when two partners take on two other players and these two players remain as permanent opponents for the entire contest.

SET UP

To establish either the dummy or a long suit by losing or ruffing out tricks.

SHADED

A bid is said to be shaded if it is slightly below the normal strength requirements.

SHAKE

A slang term for discard. See DISCARD.

SHARING BOARDS

In some movements, it is necessary for two or more tables to play the same boards on the same round. This is called "Sharing boards." Boards may be played in a different sequence as a result.

SHARK

An expert who often plays tough bridge for high stakes.

SHARPLES

A defense to 1NT whereby an overcall of 2♣ shows a hand of unspecified shape, but with at least four spades and 2♦ shows a weak distributional hand with short clubs. See DEFENSE TO 1NT.

SHIFT

1) In the auction, a change of suit as in "Jump shift."

2) In the play, a switch to another suit.

SHOOTING (FOR A TOP)

To make an apparently inferior bid or play in a deliberate attempt to score a top. The tactic is usually employed by a pair towards the end of a duplicate session in an attempt to convert a good score into a winning score.

SHORT CLUB

A prepared opening bid made on a three-card club suit. Advocates of five card major openings are likely to play the short club.

SHORTEN

To reduce in length. Commonly refers to the situation where dummy's or declarer's trumps are removed by forcing him to ruff. See PUNCH.

SHORT HAND

The hand with the fewer number of cards in a suit (usually trumps).

SHORT SUIT GAME TRIES

A game try whereby, after trump agreement, opener shows his shortest suit and invites responder to judge accordingly. See TRIAL BID.

SHORT SUIT LEADS

The lead of a short suit, usually when partner has bid the suit, but sometimes as a deceptive play hoping that declarer will think that the wrong hand has the long suit.

SHOW OUT

To reveal a void by discarding on the lead of a suit.

SHOW UP SQUEEZE (DISCLOSURE SQUEEZE)
A squeeze whiich afford declarer the luxury of refusing a losing finesse late in the play.

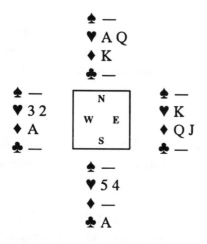

South leads the good ace of clubs and West, who is known to still possess the ace of diamonds, discards a low heart. South now leads a heart towards the dummy and West produces his last heart. Since it isn't the king, South knows that the heart finesse must fail, so he goes up with the ace in the dummy. South is well rewarded for his vigilance and technique when the heart king drops singleton.

SHUFFLE
To rearrange the cards in a more or less random way.

SHUT OUT BID
See PREEMPTIVE BID.

SIDE
A partnership in a rubber game; a duplicate game or teams of four match.

SIDE GAME
A second competition at a championship for pairs or teams not involved in the main event.

SIDE SUIT
A suit other than trumps. It is also known as a "plain suit."

SIGNALS, SIGNALLING
The method of conveying information between the defenders. This can be done both when following to a suit and when discarding.

SIGN OFF (BID)
A discouraging bid suggesting that the partnership should progress no further.

SILENT
To keep silent is to pass throughout the auction.

SILENT BIDDER
See DUMB BIDDER, WRITTEN BIDDING.

SILVER POINTS
Awarded in ACBL sectional tournaments. Among the 300 points needed to become a Life Master, at least 50 must be silver.

SIMPLE
A non-jump bid or raise when overcalling or responding.

SIMPLE FINESSE
A finesse against one outstanding card.

SIMPLE OVERCALL
A non-jump overcall.

SIMPLE SQUEEZE
Type of squeeze in which a single opponent is squeezed.

SIMPLIFIED PRECISION
A very natural version of the Precision System of bidding. See PRECISION.

SIMULTANEOUS CALL
Calls made by two players at the same time. If it was properly the turn of one of the players to call, the other is deemed to be subsequent.

SIMULTANEOUS PAIRS
Event played in many different venues on the same date and with identical hands so that nationwide or even worldwide matchpointing may be employed. See PRE-DEALING.

SIMULTANEOUS PLAY
1. When a pre-duplicated board is being played at more than one table within a section at the same time (for the purpose of instant matchpointing).
2. When two players accidentally play a card at the same time.

SINGLE COUP

Preparation for an endplay in which declarer trumps a winning card from dummy in order to shorten his trump holding to the same size as his RHO. He leads a card eventually from dummy and coups RHO out of his trump card. If declarer does his shortening twice, it would constitute a double coup, and if declarer trumps three winners, it is a triple (trump-reducing) coup.

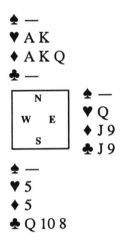

The trump position has been revealed in a club contract and East is known to have the guarded jack of clubs. Declarer must shorten his trumps to the same sssize as East and then arrange to lead from dummy at trick 12. A diamond is led to the dummy and a good diamond from dummy is then ruffed. A heart lead to dummy now allows South to lead from dummy at trick 12 and coup East out of his club position.

SINGLE DUMMY PROBLEMS

Bridge problems presented as if in the position of declarer.

SINGLE RAISE

A raise of partner's denomination by one level.

SINGLETON
A holding of one card in a suit.

SIT (FOR)
Passing partner's double. Frequently relates to situations when not everyone would pass.

SIT OUT
If there is an odd number of pairs in a duplicate event, every round one pair has no opponents and thus sits out. It also means to wait to cut in to a game of rubber bridge.

SKIP BID
See JUMP BID, STOP.

SKIP BID WARNING
Sponsoring organizations may require that a warning be given before a jump bid (skip bid) is made and require the next player to pause for a specified period before bidding. See STOP.

SKIP (ROUND)
A round during a Mitchell movement at which the East- West pairs "skip," moving two tables instead of the usual one. The boards move as normal. See MITCHELL.

SLAM
A contract for twelve (small slam) or thirteen tricks (grand slam). For bidding and making either type of slam considerable bonuses are awarded. See BONUS.

SLAM BIDDING
The various approaches to the investigation and bidding of 6 and 7 level contracts. Since the earliest days of bridge, slam bidding methods and conventions have been prevalent. Listed below are only a few of the more well-known: Culbertson 4-5 NT; Blackwood (and its many variations); Gerber; DOPI and ROPI; Cuebidding controls; Fragment bids; Splinter bids; Grand Slam Force; Trump Asking Bids; Control Asking Bids.

SLAM CONVENTION(S)
An agreed bidding convention, such as Blackwood, for checking on controls, trumps or other key cards held by the partnership to investigate slam possibilities.

SLAM DOUBLES
See LIGHTNER DOUBLE, UNPENALTY DOUBLE.

SLIDING BLACKWOOD
See ROLLING BLACKWOOD.

SLIDING GERBER
See ROLLING GERBER.

SLOW PASS
Passing after a noticeable hesitation; usually indicates that some other action was being considered. In and of itself not a violation, however, the chance of unauthorized information being made available to partner is considerable.

SLOW PLAY (PENALTY)
Any action that unduly delays or obstructs the game or inconveniences other contestants is liable to a procedural penalty. Includes (but not restricted to) comparing scores, loudness, slow play and tardiness.

SLUFF
To discard a loser; from "slough": to cast off.

SLUFF AND RUFF
See RUFF AND SLUFF.

SMALL CARD
In general, a card below honor rank, often denoted by an "x" on a hand record.

SMALL SLAM
To contract to make twelve tricks is to bid a small slam. It is sometimes called a "Little Slam ." See BONUS.

SMITH ECHO
The Smith Echo is a suit-preference signal used against notrump contracts. The purpose of the echo, by either defender, is to indicate his desire to have his partner continue the suit led on opening lead. A defender's failure to echo suggests that his partner should shift to another suit.

SMOLEN TRANSFERS
A convention designed to make the notrump opener declarer in any major suit game. Using this device, after a negative two diamond response to his Stayman inquiry, the responder's jump to three of a major suit shows specifically four cards in the suit bid, and five or six cards in the other major.

SMOTHER PLAY

A rare endplay in which a seemingly certain losing trump trick vanishes. The defending hand with trump length is reduced to trumps alone and has the choice of underruffing, thus unguarding his honor, or overuffing only to be overruffed in turn. For example:

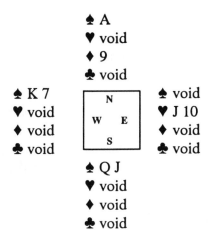

```
              ♠ A
              ♥ void
              ♦ 9
              ♣ void
   ♠ K 7                    ♠ void
   ♥ void     ┌─────────┐   ♥ J 10
   ♦ void     │    N    │   ♦ void
   ♣ void     │  W   E  │   ♣ void
             │    S    │
              └─────────┘
              ♠ Q J
              ♥ void
              ♦ void
              ♣ void
```

Spades are trumps and East, on lead, plays a heart. South, declarer, ruffs and West is subjected to a smother play or coup.

SNAP

An acronym for **S**trong **N**o Trump **A**fter **P**assing, this convention uses the response of 1NT to an opening bid of one of a suit, made by partner third or fourth in hand, to show 8 - 10 points.

SOCIAL BRIDGE

Bridge played in the home. The Chicago method of scoring has become more frequently used, although rubber bridge is still popular.

SOCK (SOCK IT)

Slang term for double.

SOFT VALUES

Queens and Jacks. By comparison, Aces and Kings are called "hard values."

SOLID

1) Describes a suit with no losers.
2) An unbeatable contract.

SORT (SORT YOUR HAND)

Separating the cards into suits and arranging the cards within the suit in some order. It is smart practice to alter your sorting methods.

SOS REDOUBLE

A redouble suggesting that an alternative denomination be chosen. See KOCK-WERNER REDOUBLE, REDOUBLE.

SOUND BIDDING

Bids of minimum or above standard.

SOUTH

One of the positions at the bridge table.

SOUTH AFRICAN TEXAS

The use of 4♣ and 4♦ bids as transfers to 4♥ and 4♠ respectively, either as opening bids or in response to 1NT / 2NT. The transfer suggests a stronger hand than bidding 4♥ or 4♠ directly. See TEXAS CONVENTION.

SPADES

1. The highest-ranking of the 4 suits. 2. The symbols (♠) on these 13 cards.

SPECTATOR

A person who watches a bridge event. The spectator may be physically present at or near the table (kibitzer) or as part of an audience viewing the event on a screen.

SPEEDBALL
An event such as a midnight zip Swiss team, which is played with less time allowed per board. The goal is to finish the event more quickly than usual. See ZIP SWISS.

SPIRAL CUE-BIDS
A device employed by the Romex System in the course of slam exploration. It is used after one member of the partnership has responded to a convention such as Roman Key Card Blackwood, disclosing his "key cards." The premise is that the response has revealed that the partnership holds all of the key cards, and the goal is disclosure of certain other cards that may be material to a grand slam.

SPLIMIT RAISES
Uses jump shifts by responder over an opponent's takeout double. They show a hand worth 9-11 points with three or four-card support for opener's suit, and with a singleton or void in the suit bid. The name "splimit" is a combination of "SPLInter," the common term for a singleton-showing bid, and "LIMIT" raise.

SPLINTER BID
A double jump response, usually to a major suit opening, showing trump support, the values for game, and a singleton or void in the suit bid. See CUE BID, FRAGMENT BID.

SPLIT
The way a suit is divided.

SPLITTING HONORS

The play of an honor, from two or more in sequence, in the second position. For example:

```
            A J 4
K Q 9                10 8 3 2
            7 6 5
```

South leads the 5 and, if West plays the King or Queen, he is said to split his honors.

SPONSOR(S)

1. Person(s) or organization(s) that contribute to or pay the cost of running a bridge tournament.

2. Person who pays a player to be his partner or to be part of a team he is backing.

SPOT CARDS

Cards from the two to the nine inclusive.

SPREAD

1) To place the cards of the dummy face up on the table.

2) To lay one's hand on the table in making a claim.

3) A term for an unbeatable contract as in "Four spades was a spread."

SPUTNIK DOUBLE

See NEGATIVE DOUBLE.

SQUARE HAND
Refers to distribution. A balanced hand, 4-3-3-3. See also FLAT HAND.

Square Hand

SQUEEZE
Descriptive term for a variety of plays where an opponent is forced to discard in a suit or suits that he wishes to guard. The end result is that the enemy makes a trick (sometimes more) that seemed unlikely at the start of play. There are a great many squeeze plays, many with set names, varying from the simple to the complex. Here are two basic ones:

1. a)

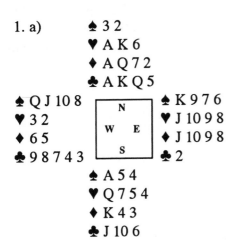

♠ 3 2
♥ A K 6
♦ A Q 7 2
♣ A K Q 5

♠ Q J 10 8
♥ 3 2
♦ 6 5
♣ 9 8 7 4 3

♠ K 9 7 6
♥ J 10 9 8
♦ J 10 9 8
♣ 2

♠ A 5 4
♥ Q 7 5 4
♦ K 4 3
♣ J 10 6

SQUEEZE (continued)

b)

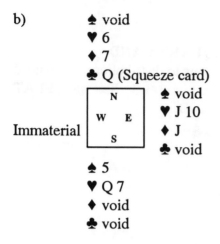

```
                ♠ void
                ♥ 6
                ♦ 7
                ♣ Q (Squeeze card)
                        ♠ void
                        ♥ J 10
Immaterial              ♦ J
                        ♣ void
                ♠ 5
                ♥ Q 7
                ♦ void
                ♣ void
```

This is the hand a) given under RECTIFYING THE COUNT. South plays in 6NT and receives the Queen of spades lead. He ducks, to rectify the count, and West continues the suit. Neither red suit breaks evenly but, since East is guarding both of them, the position in b) develops. When North's winning club is led East has no safe discard.

2. a)

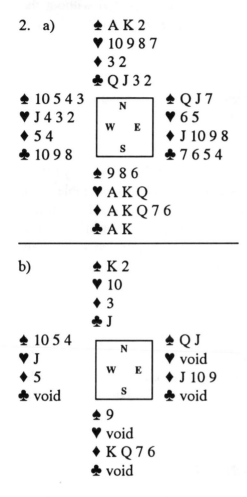

```
              ♠ A K 2
              ♥ 10 9 8 7
              ♦ 3 2
              ♣ Q J 3 2
♠ 10 5 4 3                      ♠ Q J 7
♥ J 4 3 2        N             ♥ 6 5
♦ 5 4         W     E          ♦ J 10 9 8
♣ 10 9 8         S             ♣ 7 6 5 4
              ♠ 9 8 6
              ♥ A K Q
              ♦ A K Q 7 6
              ♣ A K
```

b)

```
              ♠ K 2
              ♥ 10
              ♦ 3
              ♣ J
♠ 10 5 4                       ♠ Q J
♥ J            N               ♥ void
♦ 5         W     E            ♦ J 10 9
♣ void         S              ♣ void
              ♠ 9
              ♥ void
              ♦ K Q 7 6
              ♣ void
```

South plays in 7NT and West leads the 10 of clubs. There are twelve top tricks and if either red suit breaks 3 - 3 there will be no problem. The heart suit fails to work but South gives himself an extra chance by arriving in position b). East has already discarded a club on a heart and, when North's Jack of clubs is led, must discard a spade. South throws a diamond. When South now wins K Q of diamonds, West must either discard a spade or a heart. Either is fatal. This is known as a double squeeze.

SQUEEZE WITHOUT THE COUNT
Term used for a squeeze which can be executed without the requirement to rectify the count. See RECTIFYING THE COUNT.

STACKED (STACK)
The cards are said to be stacked when a single opponent holds all or nearly all the crucial cards in a given suit.

STAKES
The unit of monetary consideration per point in a money bridge game. If the stakes are a penny a point, a non-vulnerable set of down one (or 50 points) is worth 50¢. A vulnerable slam in a major suit is worth (1430 points) or $14.30. At bridge clubs throughout the world where they play money bridge, stakes vary from a quarter of a cent a point to $5 a point or more.

STAND (A DOUBLE)
To pass partner's double.

STANDARD AMERICAN
Nebulous term for bidding methods common in the U.S., approximately those that were originally laid down by Charles H. Goren.

STANDARD HONOR LEADS
See LEADING FROM HONORS.

STAND OFF
No net difference in the score, applied to rubber and team matches.

STAND UP
A high card that wins a trick. A suit led by the defense may stand up until it is ruffed by the declarer.

STANZA

A set of boards played before scoring or moving to another table.

Sam Stayman

STAYMAN CONVENTION

A 2♣ response to a 1NT opening bid, used to enquire about major suit holdings. In response, opener rebids:

2♦   No four card major.
2♥   Four hearts (and possibly four spades).
2♠   Four spades.

See EXTENDED STAYMAN, PUPPET STAYMAN, STAYMAN THREE CLUBS.

STAYMAN IN DOUBT (SID)

After a positive response to the 2♣ inquiry (2♠ / 2♥), a bid of 3♦ indicates a four card fit in the bid major, values for game but a 4 - 3 - 3 - 3 or 3 - 4 - 3 - 3 hand pattern. Partner chooses either to bid four of the major or 3NT depending on his hand pattern. Duplication of distribution may mean that 3NT is an easier game contract despite the 4 - 4 major suit fit.

STAYMAN THREE CLUBS

The use of 3♣ in response to a 2NT opening to enquire about four card majors in the same way that 2♣ is used in response to 1NT.

STEPPINGSTONE SQUEEZE

A squeeze in which declarer first forces a defender to keep his guard in a suit; declarer then throws him in and forces him to lead that suit.

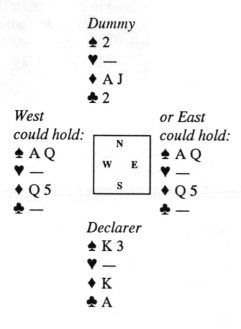

Dummy
♠ 2
♥ —
♦ A J
♣ 2

West could hold:
♠ A Q
♥ —
♦ Q 5
♣ —

or East could hold:
♠ A Q
♥ —
♦ Q 5
♣ —

Declarer
♠ K 3
♥ —
♦ K
♣ A

South needs three tricks. First, he cashes the ace of clubs. If either defender has the ace of spades and the guarded queen of diamonds, he's in trouble. Since he can't part with a low diamond (because declarer would then overtake his king with dummy's ace, felling the queen of diamonds), the defender must bare down to the stiff ace of spades. He is then thrown in with that card after South cashes the king of diamonds. All the defender has left is the queen of diamonds which he must now lead to dummy's ace of diamonds.

STEP RESPONSES
System of responses, especially to an artificial bid such as a 2♣ opening, or a Blackwood 4NT inquiry, whereby the number of features (Aces, controls, points etc.) is shown by steps.

STIFF
Singleton, usually a high honor card, as in "The stiff King."

STOP
A method of alerting opponents that a player is about to make a jump bid. A player who is about to make a jump bid precedes his bid with the words "Stop" or "Skip bid." The next player should then pause for some five to ten seconds before bidding. See JUMP BID, SKIP BID WARNING.

STOP BID
A bid finalizing the auction and asking partner to stop bidding. If partner opens the bidding with 1 NT (you are not playing transfer bids) and you hold ♠ J96432 ♥ 72 ♦ 83 ♣ K43, you know that your hand should probably be played in spades rather than notrump. You would bid two spades (a stop or "drop dead" bid). Partner should honor your request and stop bidding. With ♠ KQJ632 ♥ K4 ♦ 96 ♣ 932 you would make a different stop bid of four spades over partner's 1 NT opening bid. 1 NT - pass - 3 NT by you also asks partner to stop bidding.

STOPLIGHT
Based on the use of a three club bid as an artificial, presumably weak, rebid after a game-invitational jump to two notrump. The three club bid is used to allow the partnership to play in suit contracts below the game level.

STOPPER (A STOP)
A holding that prevents the immediate run of a suit.

STOPPING BELOW GAME
When a partnership intentionally or accidentally fails to reach the game level.

Stopping on a Dime.

STOPPING ON A DIME
Failing to reach a game (or maybe a slam) and stopping at precisely the perfect level (2 NT, for instance, taking exactly 8 tricks).

STRAIN
Any one of the four suits or notrump. The level and strain of the contract are determined by the bidding.

STRIP (PLAY)
To strip a player of safe exit cards, so that when the defender is thrown in he cannot help but concede a trick.

STRIPED-TAILED APE DOUBLE
A double of a game (or slam) contract in the expectation that the opponents could make a slam (or grand slam) and in the hope that they will accept the, apparently, good score for making a doubled game (or slam) with overtricks rather than go on to the higher scoring slam (or grand slam). The convention is so named because the doubler flees like a striped-tailed ape in the face of a redouble.

Stripe-Trailed Ape Double.

STRONG JUMP OVERCALLS
A single jump overcall showing a good six card suit and about 15-17 high card points.

STRONG KINGS AND TENS
A system of honor leads against a no trump contract whereby the lead of a King or 10 suggests a strong holding, and the lead of an Ace, Queen or Jack suggests a relatively weak holding.

Ace from:	A K x
King from:	A K Q, A K J, A K 10, K Q J, K Q 10
Queen from:	K Q x, K Q 9, Q J 10
Jack from:	J 10 x
Ten from:	A J 10, A 10 9, K J 10, K 10 9, Q 10 9
Nine from:	10 9 x

See LEADING FROM HONORS.

STRONG MINOR RAISE
See INVERTED MINOR SUIT RAISES.

STRONG NO TRUMP
An opening 1NT bid with usually 15-17 or 16-18 points and a balanced hand.

STRONG NO TRUMP AFTER PASSING
See SNAP.

STRONG PASS (SYSTEMS)
Systems featuring an opening pass in first or second position to show about 16+ points.

STRONG TWO BID

A bid that shows substantial playing strength in the suit named (as in Acol) or is forcing to game (as in Standard American). In Acol, the openings of 2♦, 2♥ and 2♠ show at least eight playing tricks and at least a six card suit or a powerful 5 - 5 two-suited hand.

Strong Two Bid

SUBSTITUTE BOARD

A replacement board in a team game. It is ordered by the director when he deems that no normal result is possible, because of some irregularity occurring on the original board.

SUBSTITUTE CALL

One replacing an illegal bid. A player may substitute a legal call with possible penalties against his partner under bridge laws.

SUBSTITUTE PLAYER

1. In rubber bridge, one who sits in for a departed player during a rubber.

2. In duplicate bridge, one approved by the director to finish a session or sessions in the place of a participant unable to finish the game.

SUCKER DOUBLE

A double made by a player relying on his high card values alone to set a contract. On distributional hands, tricks based on outside aces and kings can evaporate because of short suits in declarer's hand or the dummy. In freely bid games, the shortness in side suits is considered in the bidding, so beware of making a double which might tip off your holdings for a possible small profit. Also be wary of doubling with strong trump holdings, lest the declarer (duly warned) play the trump suit in an other-than-usual manner and negate your holding.

SUFFICIENT BID

A bid at a higher level than the previous bid or at the same level in a higher ranking denomination.

SUICIDE SQUEEZE

The play when a defender, rather than declarer, leads the card that squeezes partner.

SUIT

Method of categorizing the fifty-two cards in a pack, identified by the shape of the pip spades, hearts, diamonds or clubs.

SUIT COMBINATION(S)

The way the cards in a particular suit are divided, such as: A108 in the dummy and KJ9753 in declarer's hand. It is most helpful to the aspiring bridge student to learn the best way to handle various suit combinations. This is a very complex topic. In the "Official Encyclopedia of Bridge" (1984 edition) 56 pages are devoted to this subject.

Suit Combinations

SUIT PATTERN

How the 13 cards are divided between the four hands at the table, ranging from 4-4-3-2 (the most likely) to 13-0-0-0 (the least likely). A particular player's suit pattern refers to how his suits are divided within his hand. If a player has four spades, five hearts, two diamonds and two clubs, he is said to hold a 4-5-2-2 hand or (if you wish to disregard the order of hierarchy) a 5-4-2-2- hand.

SUIT PREFERENCE SIGNAL

Defensive signal whereby the play of the cards in one suit is used to indicate preference between two other suits. See McKENNEY, REVOLVING DISCARDS, LAVINTHAL DISCARDS.

SUPER BLACKWOOD

In sequences when 4 NT would be natural, a bid of four in the lowest unbid suit asks for aces.

SUPER PRECISION ASKING BIDS

In the Super Precision System of bidding, a number of different types of asking bids are used. The opener can ask about the quality of a suit bid by the responder, about the responder's high card or distributional controls, or about the responder's support for the opener's suit. They are named after Greek letters (Alpha, Beta, etc.).

SUPPORT

    1) To raise partner's suit.
    2) A worthwhile holding in partner's suit.

SUPPORT DOUBLES

A device used by some partnerships to allow opener to show support for responder's suit, notwithstanding an intervening overcall and to differentiate between good and mediocre holdings in the suit.

SUPPRESSING THE BID ACE
To ignore an already identified Ace (such as by a cue bid) in responding to Blackwood.

SURE TRICK
A trick that a player is certain to make.

SURPLUS CARDS
More than 13 cards in one hand.

SURROUNDING PLAY
Maneuver in which a defender breaks a suit by leading a high card that is part of a near-sequential holding.

SWING
The net difference in the score on a board in a teams of four match.

SWING HAND
A hand on which a large swing occurred or which had the potential for a large swing.

SWINDLES
Legal ways to deceive the opponents such as false cards in the play and psychic bids.

SWISH
Passed out, such as "1♥ – Pass – 4♥ - Swish."

SWISS CONVENTION

A convention whereby responses of 4♣ or 4♦ to an opening of one of a major show a good fit, sound values for game and some interest in a slam, thus releasing the direct raise to four of opener's major to be used pre-emptively. There are many versions of Swiss. The three most popular are:

SINGLETON SWISS

    4♣   Shows two Aces and a singleton. 4♦ from partner asks responder to identify the singleton.

    4♦   Shows two Aces without a singleton.

FRUIT MACHINE SWISS (THREE WAY SWISS)

    4♣   Shows either two Aces and a singleton, or three Aces, or two Aces and the King of trumps. 4♦ from opener is then a relay requesting clarification. In reply, 4NT shows three Aces, a bid of four of the agreed trump suit shows two Aces and the trump King, and a new suit shows two Aces and a singleton in the suit bid.

    4♦   Shows two Aces without any of the features shown by the 4♣ response.

TRUMP SWISS

    4♣   Shows good controls.
    4♦   Shows good trumps.

More complex versions of Swiss (e.g. Super Swiss) use conventional responses of 3NT and a double jump in the unbid major in addition to the responses of 4♣ and 4♦. In conjunction with further relays they allow responder to make very fine distinctions between different types of raises. See MINOR SUIT SWISS.

SWISS PAIRS

A competition for a large number of pairs whereby a few short matches are played and at every stage the two leading pairs are drawn against each other, subject to their not having met previously. Similarly the third and fourth placed pairs oppose each other etc.

SWISS TEAMS (SWISS MOVEMENT)

A competition for teams organized in the same way as for Swiss Pairs. See TEAM OF FOUR.

SWITCH

    1) To lead a different suit from the one previously being led.

    2) Arrow switch, an adaptation towards the end of a session allowing a single winner to be determined from a Mitchell movement.

See MITCHELL, SCRAMBLED MITCHELL.

SWORDS

One of the suits on cards when spades, hearts, etc., are not used.

SYMMETRY OF DISTRIBUTION
(LAW OF SYMMETRY)

Culbertson assumed that from the character of his own hand pattern a player can draw inferences concerning the pattern of the other hands and the distribution of the four suits. Culbertson contended:

    1. That a player who held a hand of a special pattern could expect one of the other three players to hold a similar pattern.

    2. That a player's hand pattern was likely to be reproduced in the distribution of at least one of the suits, usually his longest suit.

    This theory has no mathematical basis.

SYSTEM
The total framework in which the partnership assigns well-defined meanings to its bids and bidding sequences.

SYSTEM FIX
An unfortunate result caused by the bidding system or convention you are playing.

ℭ

TABLE

1) A team of four, two pairs or four players in a duplicate event.

2) The dummy.

3) To table one's hand it to expose it, either as dummy or when making a claim.

Table

TABLE FEEL (TABLE PRESENCE)

The ability to draw inferences from the extraneous things that happen at the table.

TABLE GUIDE CARD (GUIDE CARD)

A card placed on each table instructing players which table to move to after each round. See HOWELL, MITCHELL.

TABLE MANNERS

Correct behavior.

TABLE NUMBERS

Numbered cards placed on each table for identification purposes.

TABLING DUMMY

At the end of the auction when partner is the declarer, placing your hand face up on the table.

Tabling Dummy

TACTICS

The various methods used in the auction and the play of the hand. As in a military situation, one side's tactics depend on the other side's actions.

TAKE OUT

A bid in a denomination other than that previously bid by partner. See WEAK TAKE OUT.

TAKE OUT DOUBLE

A double which is used conventionally to ask partner to bid his best suit. Traditionally a double is defined as being for take out if it is: 1) of a suit bid at the one or two level, 2) made at the first opportunity to double that suit, 3) made before partner has bid. See BALANCING, DOUBLE.

TALLIES
Scoring sheets to record results for progressive or party bridge.

TANK, TO GO INTO THE
To pause for a long time when faced with a difficult decision in bidding or play.

TAP
To gently knock the table:

    1) A method of alerting partner's conventional bid.

    2) In rubber bridge, to pass (although this is technically not a legal call).

    3) Make a player ruff, attempting to have him lose trump control.

TARTAN TWO BIDS
Multicolored openings of Scottish origin in which an opening bid of two hearts or two spades shows either an Acol-two bid in the suit opened, or a weak two-suited hand that includes the suit opened.

TEAM
A group of four or more players competing as a single unit.

TEAMMATES
The other pair or pairs on the team.

TEAM OF FOUR
Two pairs playing in different directions at different tables, but for a common score. See SWISS TEAMS.

Team of Four

TEAM TRIALS

Event held annually in Memphis to determine the U.S. representatives in the World Championships.

TEMPO

1) To have the initiative in the play. For example:

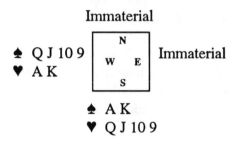

West on lead against South's no trump contract has the initiative (tempo) and can guarantee four tricks by leading his long suit.

2) In bidding or play, the general rhythm of a player's actions. See RHYTHM.

TEMPORIZE

Bid a suit (often, an unplayable suit), in the expectation of supporting partner's suit later. May be required if no immediate raise is appropriate.

TEMPORIZING BID

See WAITING BID.

TENACE

A holding of two (normally high) cards in the same suit, one ranking next above and the other next below a card held by an opponent, e.g. A Q or K J. A holding which is not strictly a tenace before play starts may become one during the course of play. For example, A J x opposite x x x becomes a tenace if the King is led. See MAJOR TENACE, MINOR TENACE.

TEXAS CONVENTION (TEXAS TRANSFER)
A transfer method in response to a 1NT / 2NT opening bid. In response, a jump to 4♦ is a transfer to 4♥ and a bid of 4♥ a transfer to 4♠. See SOUTH AFRICAN TEXAS.

THIN
1) A contract bid on very slender values.
2) A hand too weak for a specific action.

THIRD
Descriptive of the number of cards held in a suit. If you wish to talk about the hand: ♠ A43 ♥ A ♦ 8653 ♣ AQ763, you might describe it as "Ace third, ace singleton, four little and ace queen fifth."

THIRD AND FIFTH LEADS
A convention whereby, from long suits without an honor sequence, the third highest card is led from three and four card suits and the fifth highest is led from longer holdings.

THIRD HAND
In the auction, dealer's partner. In the play, leader's partner.

THIRD HAND HIGH
A whist rule suggesting that the correct action to take when one's partner has led is to play one's highest card (but the lowest of equals).

THIRD IN HAND OPENER (THIRD SEAT OPENER)
In the third seat it can be good tactics to open on a hand that is slightly below the usual strength for an opening bid. Such an opening is called a third in hand opener.

THIRTEENER
The one remaining card in a suit after all of the others have been played.

THREAT CARD (MENACE)
A card which, while not yet a winner, may become established as a winner if the opponents can be forced to weaken their holding in the suit. The term is principally used in connection with squeezes. See ISOLATING THE MENACE, SQUEEZE.

THREE HANDED BRIDGE
Originally devised by three players unable to locate a fourth, there have been many variations through the years. In "Cutthroat Bridge" the three players bid for the privilege of partnering a hidden dummy. The auction continues until a bid is followed by two passes. The person sitting to the left of the high bidder then makes an opening lead. The dummy is revealed and placed opposite the high bidder. Scoring is normal. "TRIO," another three-handed game, was concocted by George Coffin in 1932. In this game each player partners a pre-exposed dummy for an entire rubber, the cards being shuffled after each hand.

THREE NO TRUMP FOR TAKE OUT
A convention whereby an overcall of 3NT after an opponent's three level pre-emptive opening is a take out request. See DEFENSE TO OPENING THREE BID.

THREE OF THE HOUSE
Colloquialism for 3NT.

THREE QUARTER MOVEMENT
A Howell movement when not all the pairs meet. See HOWELL.

THREE QUARTER NO TRUMP
To play a strong no trump only when vulnerable against non-vulnerable opponents, with a weak no trump at other times.

THREE SUITER
A hand with four or more cards in three suits i.e. 4 - 4 - 4 - 1 or 5 - 4 - 4 - 0.

THROUGH STRENGTH
See LEAD THROUGH STRENGTH.

THROW AWAY
To discard.

THROW IN
1) A deal when all four players pass.

2) To deliberately give a player the lead with the expectation of a favorable return. See EXIT CARD.

TICKETS
1. A slang term for high cards, such as "He was dealt all the tickets."

2. Pick-up slips in a duplicate event.

TIE
1. (on a board) — Scores equal to each other.

2. (In a knockout match) — If there is no clear-cut winner of a knockout match after the prescribed number of boards, the match must be resolved by playing an abbreviated playoff.

3. (In scores placing within a section or in overall standings) — Prior to 1992, the ACBL judged two scores to be tied if they were less than .50 apart. Now, a score of even .01 ahead of the other score results in a clear victory.

TIGHT
1. A contract close to failure.

2. Slang for a singleton or doubleton.

TIMING
The order in which a hand is planned and played. Declarer and defenders must consider such factors as drawing trump, ruffing losers and developing suits within the scenario of each hand.

TOP
Highest matchpoint score available on each board in a duplicate pairs event.

TOP AND BOTTOM CUE-BIDS
Require that the cue-bidder's two suits be the highest unbid suit and the lowest unbid suit.

TOP OF NOTHING (LEAD)
Standard lead with a holding of two or three small cards (and sometimes more).

TOTAL POINT SCORING
Form of scoring at teams whereby the team with the largest aggregate score wins.

TOUCHING CARDS
Cards in sequence.

TOUCHING HONORS
Two or more high cards within a suit, each with equal value, i.e., Q J 10. When you *lead* from such a holding, choose the *top* one (the Q). When you *follow suit* (if you are the second or third one to play on a trick), *play* the *lower* or *lowest* (the ten). When your 10 dislodges the king or the ace, partner will know that you might have the intermediate cards. If you mistakenly play the queen rather than the ten, thinking that you are bamboozling the declarer, you'll merely end up fooling partner, who will never figure you for the jack and the ten.

TOUCHING SUITS
Clubs and diamonds, diamonds and hearts, hearts and spades, and spades and clubs are said to be touching suits.

TOURNAMENT
Any competitive bridge event, ranging from a local duplicate game to a National championship. The ABA and the ACBL sponsor hundreds of sectional, regional and national tournaments each year.

TOURNAMENT COMMITTEE
(TOURNAMENT CHAIRPERSON)
Persons within the sponsoring organization responsible fur the running and success of a tournament. Usually there are two areas of concern, preparation and operation. The preparations include such concerns as site selection, prizes, sanction procuring, selecting directors, dates, publicity, player activities and financing. During the operation of the tournament, the concerns of the committee are mainly partnership, hospitality and appeals.

TOURNAMENT DIRECTOR

Person delegated by the sponsoring organization to see to the smooth running of the tournament, to give rulings on points of law and to sort out any irregularities.

TOWIE

A three-handed bridge game, but it is actually intended for at least one or two additional people to be involved. Only three players participate at one time.

TRAM TICKETS

Very poor cards.

TRANCE

To pause for a substantial length of time during bidding or play.

TRANSFER BIDS

Bids of suits which show the suit ranking immediately above that which is bid and request partner to bid that suit. They are most commonly used after partner opens 1NT or 2NT and allow greater flexibility in the bidding. The basic principle is that with, for example, a five card or longer heart suit, one responds in diamonds. Partner will convert to hearts after which responder may pass with a weak hand, or make some further descriptive bid. See JACOBY TRANSFERS, SOUTH AFRICAN TEXAS, TEXAS CONVENTION.

TRANSFERRED TRICK
After a revoke has been established, a trick which had been won by the offending side may have to be transfered back to the opponents.

TRANSFERRING THE MENACE
Method of changing which opponent guards a particular suit in order that a squeeze can be executed. See SQUEEZE, THREAT CARD (MENACE).

TRANSFER SQUEEZE
An exotic squeeze in which one defender is squeezed late in the hand, because control of a suit is transferred to him by the resourceful declarer's handling of the cards. Take this case:

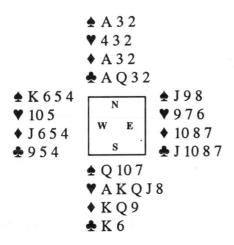

```
                  ♠ A 3 2
                  ♥ 4 3 2
                  ♦ A 3 2
                  ♣ A Q 3 2
  ♠ K 6 5 4                   ♠ J 9 8
  ♥ 10 5          N           ♥ 9 7 6
  ♦ J 6 5 4     W   E         ♦ 10 8 7
  ♣ 9 5 4         S           ♣ J 10 8 7
                  ♠ Q 10 7
                  ♥ A K Q J 8
                  ♦ K Q 9
                  ♣ K 6
```

West leads a low diamond against 7 NT. South has 12 tricks on top and the 13th must come from a black suit squeeze. Declarer's best chance is to cash his ace of spades and then run all of his side suit winners in the red suits. If either opponent was dealt the king of spades and four clubs, he will be squeezed. It fails on this hand. However, should South take a less likely percentage play by leading the queen of spades from his hand early and West covers with the king, this would transfer the guardianship of the spade trick to East's jack. When South now runs his red cards, East throws in the towel, being unable to keep his spade jack and four clubs.

TRAP (TRAP PASS)
To pass holding a strong hand in the hope the opposition will overbid and a substantial penalty can be extracted.

TRAVELLER OR TRAVELLING SCORESLIP
The slip of paper which accompanies a board as it travels round the room in a duplicate event on which the result of each pair that has played played the hand is recorded. See PICK UP SLIP, SCORESLIP.

OFFICIAL (Mitchell or Howell) TRAVELING SCORE

Bid, play and score this board without comment and proceed immediately to the next.
NORTH PLAYER only keeps score

ENTER PAIR NO. OF E-W PAIR   Board No. _____

N-S Pair	E-W Pair	CON-TRACT	BY	MADE	DOWN	FINAL SCORE North South	East West	E-W Match Points	N-S Match Points
1									
2									
3									
4									
5									
6									
7									
8							1		
9							2		
10							3		
11							4		
12							5		
13							6		
14							7		

Indulge in post-mortems, if you must, only at end of round. Play congenially. Announce or display private conventions. Refrain from giving lessons, especially to opponents. Do not make your own rulings; call your game director, that's his job. Count your cards before and after.
BARON BARCLAY BRIDGE SUPPLIES   #7274
1-800-274-2221

TRAY
1) A device which was used before the advent of duplicate boards to hold the fifty-two cards in 4 groups of 13, one group for each player.

2) Currently, a device used in major championships along with bidding boxes and screens, to ensure the most ethical game possible.

TREATMENT
That part of an agreed system designed to handle certain situations that arise in the bidding. It may also be a variation of a particular convention.

TREY
The 3 of each suit.

TRIAL BID
A bid in a new suit after trumps have been agreed as a suggestion that game be bid if partner has an appropriate holding in the context of his previous bidding, with particular reference to his holding in the trial bid suit. See SHORT SUIT GAME TRIES.

TRICK
The lead, and three subsequent cards, played in rotation.

Trick

TRICK POINTS
Points recorded below the line in rubber bridge.

TRICK SCORE
Points scored by declarer's side for fulfilling the contract.

TRIPLE RAISE
A raise missing out two levels of bidding. It is usually pre-emptive in nature.

TRIPLE SQUEEZE
A squeeze against one opponent in three suits.

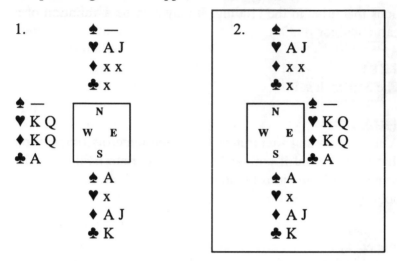

1.
```
              ♠ —
              ♥ A J
              ♦ x x
              ♣ x
♠ —        ┌─────────┐
♥ K Q      │    N    │
♦ K Q      │ W     E │
♣ A        │    S    │
           └─────────┘
              ♠ A
              ♥ x
              ♦ A J
              ♣ K
```

2.
```
              ♠ —
              ♥ A J
              ♦ x x
              ♣ x
           ┌─────────┐    ♠ —
           │    N    │    ♥ K Q
           │ W     E │    ♦ K Q
           │    S    │    ♣ A
           └─────────┘
              ♠ A
              ♥ x
              ♦ A J
              ♣ K
```

In 1. when South leads the ace of spades, West has no recourse. In fact, West must give up a heart to prevent South from winning all five tricks.

In 2. East is now the squeezee and nothing can prevent declarer from taking all the tricks. Whatever suit East is squeezed out of by the ace of spades, declarer now cashes out in. This causes East to be squeezed in the remaining two suits. This type of triple squeeze is called a repeating or progressive squeeze.

TRIPLETON
A holding of three cards in a suit.

TRUMP (TRUMPS)
A card in the trump suit as determined by the last suit bid in the auction.

TRUMP ASKING BID
A bid which inquires as to the quality of partner's trump holding. See ASKING BID, GRAND SLAM FORCE, ALPHA ASKING BID, BETA ASKING BID, DELTA ASKING BID.

TRUMP CONTROL

The player with the longest trump holding in one hand is said to have trump control. When two players have equally long trump suits, then the player whose partnership has the lead has the tempo and therefore trump control. See TEMPO.

TRUMP COUP

A stratagem whereby an opponent's finessable trumps are trapped without an actual finesse being taken. For example:

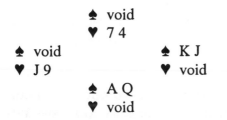

```
                ♠ void
                ♥ 7 4
  ♠ void                    ♠ K J
  ♥ J 9                     ♥ void
                ♠ A Q
                ♥ void
```

With spades as trumps, South, declarer, leads a heart from dummy. See GRAND COUP.

TRUMP ECHO

A high-low signal in the trump suit, usually used to show three trumps and/or an interest in obtaining a ruff.

TRUMP KING

Often regarded as a "fifth" Ace in control showing bids.

TRUMP PETER

See TRUMP ECHO.

TRUMP PROMOTION

To promote a trump trick in a defender's hand. This can occur basically two ways:

    1) A plain suit card is led through declarer, allowing partner to make an extra trump trick. See COUP EN PASSANT.

    2) A defender ruffs with a high trump, forcing declarer to overruff higher thus promoting a trump trick for partner. See UP-PERCUT.

Trump Promotion.

TRUMP REDUCTION PLAY

Play designed to reduce the number of trumps held by ruffing, usually in preparation for a trump coup or endplay.

TRUMP SIGNAL

An agreed method by defenders, when following in trumps, to show information in that suit or another suit. See TRUMP ECHO.

Trump Squeeze

TRUMP SQUEEZE

Squeeze in which the ability to ruff plays an essential role. The intended victim is forced to retain an extra guard to a stopper in order to protect it from being ruffed out.

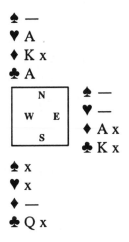

♠ —
♥ A
♦ K x
♣ A

♠ —
♥ —
♦ A x
♣ K x

♠ x
♥ x
♦ —
♣ Q x

Wiith spades as trump, South leads to the ace of hearts. If East discards a club, South cashes the ace of clubs, ruffs a diamond and wins the queen of clubs. If East discards the small diamond (the extra guard), South ruffs a diamond and returns to dummy with the ace of clubs to cash the king of diamonds.

TRUMP SUIT

The denomination of the last suit bid in the auction.

TRUMP STACK
See STACKED.

TRUMP SUPPORT
Support for partner in his proposed trump suit.

TRUMP TRICK
A trick in which the trump suit has been led.

TRUSCOTT
The Truscott convention, devised by Alan Truscott, is a system of two-suited overcalls used principally over strong artificial club and diamond opening bids.

TURKEY
Uncomplimentary term referring to less-respected players or events (such as a consolation game).

TURN
The proper time for a player to call or play.

TWINNING
Making one or more exact copies of each original deal, so that a set of boards may be played by more than one section.

TWO CLUB OPENING
In many systems, 2♣ is a strong, forcing, artificial opening. There are, however, other possibilities. It can be:
1. Strong and forcing with clubs.
2. Intermediate with clubs.
3. Intermediate showing a two-suiter.
4. A weak two.

TWO CLUB SYSTEMS
Systems employing a strong and forcing 2♣ opening bid. See CAB.

TWO DIAMOND OPENING

More meanings have been attached to 2♦ than any other opening bid. Some of the possibilities are:
  a) Weak two in diamonds.
  b) Weak two in a major.
  c) Either a weak two in a major or certain very strong hands.
  d) Intermediate with diamonds.
  e) Intermediate showing a two-suiter with diamonds.
  f) Intermediate showing hearts and spades (Flannery).
  g) Intermediate showing a three-suiter.
  h) Strong and forcing with diamonds.
  i) Strong, forcing and artificial.

TWO HEART OPENING

Most commonly played as a weak two, but as with other two level openers, it is somewhat flexible. Usually natural (with at least 5 hearts). A few conventions do exist which use 2♥ as the opening bid, such as Flannery.

TWO NO TRUMP OVERCALL

A balanced hand of some defined strength, but frequently played as a conventional bid. See UNUSUAL NO TRUMP.

TWO OVER ONE

To respond, without jumping, to partner's one level opening bid at the two level. The bid requires greater values than a one level response.

$12.95

TWO OVER ONE GAME FORCE

REVISED – EXPANDED
UPDATED FOR THE 1980s

MAX HARDY

TWO OVER ONE GAME FORCE

Bidding system based on the idea that responder's two level response (in a lower ranking suit) to opener's one bid is forcing to game. It is the most prevalent system in use in North America today.

TWO SPADE OPENING
It is most commonly played as a weak two, and sometimes as a strong two. 2♠ is not used much for artificial openings.

TWO-SUITED OPENINGS
Opening bids which show two suits, such as the Flannery Two Diamonds. See FLANNERY.

TWO-SUITED OVERCALLS
Conventional overcalls which show two suits, at least one of which is specified. See ROMAN JUMP OVERCALL.

TWO SUITER
A hand with at least five cards in each of two suits.

TWO-WAY FINESSE
A card combination allowing declarer to finesse either opponent for a missing honor. For example:

A J 10 9

K 8 7 6

With the above card combination, declarer has the choice of finessing either opponent for the missing Queen.

TWO WAY STAYMAN
The use of 2♣ as non-forcing Stayman and 2♦ as game forcing Stayman. Also known as Double-Barrelled Stayman. See STAYMAN CONVENTION.

ULTIMATE CLUB
The Ultimate Club System is based on a strong artificial one club opening bid and the availability of relay requences in every type of auction. Each opening bid at the one or two level is carefully defined in terms of distribution, strength, and controls.

UNASSUMING CUE BID
The use of a cue bid in the opponent's suit, in response to an overcall by partner, to show at least a sound minimum raise of partner's suit. This releases direct raises to be used competitively or pre-emptively. See CUE BID.

UNAUTHORIZED INFORMATION
Information available to a player which he is ethically bound not to act upon.

UNBALANCED DISTRIBUTION (UNBALANCED HAND)
Distribution which is not one of the balanced (4 - 3 - 3 - 3, 4 - 4 - 3 - 2 or 5 - 3 - 3 - 2) hand patterns.

UNBEATABLE
A contract that cannot be beaten. One which is "frigid" or "cold."

UNBID SUIT
A suit not bid during the auction period.

UNBLOCKING (PLAY)

The play of an unnecessarily high card in a suit to preserve a small card. For example:

A K J 3 2   Q 5 4

If West leads the Ace followed by the King, East must unblock the Queen in order that West can run the suit.

UNBLOCKING SQUEEZE

This particular squeeze is rare, because although the declarer has the last tricks in high cards, suit blockage makes him unable to cash them. The unblocking squeeze comes to the rescue:

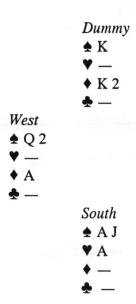

Dummy
♠ K
♥ —
♦ K 2
♣ —

West
♠ Q 2
♥ —
♦ A
♣ —

South
♠ A J
♥ A
♦ —
♣ —

In notrump, South leads the ace of hearts needing all three tricks. West must retain the ace of diamonds, lest dummy's king would become good. Therefore, West releases a low spade. South now leads his ace of spades, dropping West's queen and dummy's king. The jack of spades in the South hand is now good for the last trick.

UNDER
To be under another player is to be on his right: e.g. West is under North.

UNDERBID
To make a bid suggesting a weaker hand than that actually held.

UNDERBIDDER
One who frequently underbids.

UNDERLEAD
To lead a small card from a holding including a high card.

UNDERRUFF
To discard a small trump under the ruffing card of an opponent. This unusual play may be to avoid being endplayed or simply because a discard in a side suit cannot be afforded.

UNDER THE GUN
In the bidding or in the play, a player who is under the gun is positioned in front of a proven or potentially powerful hand.

Under the Gun

UNDERTRICK
Each trick by which declarer fails in his contract.

UNFINISHED RUBBER
If a rubber is terminated while still undecided, a side with a partial score is awarded an additional 100 points and a side with the only game receives a bonus of 300 points.

— 261 —

UNIT

The backbone of the ACBL, these local groups belong to larger districts. A unit has the right to rule over its own members, while still operating under the sovereignty of the ACBL. A unit must consist of at least 100 members.

UNLIMITED BID

A bid (such as the Acol 2♣ opener) with no upper limit.

UNMAKABLE

A contract which, if the defense is somewhat competent, should not be successful.

UNPENALTY DOUBLE

A conventional double of a slam contract showing no defensive tricks, thus allowing partner to judge whether to sacrifice. With one or more defensive tricks, one should pass. See DOUBLE.

UNUSUAL NO TRUMP

A convention whereby a bid in no trumps which, given the previous bidding, could not logically be natural, is used instead to show length in the two lowest ranking unbid suits. The most popular application is as an immediate overcall of a suit opening although, strictly, this is an extension of the convention, for such a bid could logically be natural.

UNUSUAL-OVER-UNUSUAL

An artificial method of defending against the Unusual No Trump convention. See UNUSUAL NO TRUMP.

UNUSUAL POSITIVE

In the Precision Club System, these artificial jump responses to one club show 4-4-4-1 distributions.

Uppercut

UPPERCUT
To ruff high in order to try to promote a trump trick for partner.
For example:

$\spadesuit$ 5 4 3

$\spadesuit$ J 6 $\spadesuit$ Q 2

$\spadesuit$ A K 10 9 8 7

With spades as trumps, West leads a suit in which both East and South are void and East ruffs with the Queen of spades. Assuming South overruffs, West's Jack is promoted. See TRUMP PROMOTION.

UPSIDE DOWN SIGNALS / DISCARDS
See REVERSE SIGNALS / DISCARDS.

UP THE LINE
In ascending consecutive rank order, as in "To bid four card suits up the line."

UP TO STRENGTH
    1) In the auction, having full values for a bid.
    2) In the play, the opposite of leading up to weakness.
See LEAD UP TO WEAKNESS, LEAD THROUGH STRENGTH.

UP TO WEAKNESS
See LEAD UP TO WEAKNESS, LEAD THROUGH STRENGTH.

USEFUL SPACE PRINCIPLE
This is a bidding theory set forth by Jeff Rubens in a series of articles in the *Bridge World* magazine, "Available bidding space should be assigned by a system to those devices that can best use it."

VALET
Origin of the modern day Jack, also called knave. The meaning of knave is male servant which is similar to a valet.

VALUE OF GAME
Knowing when to bid a game is difficult to calculate at the table. The chance of success to justify bidding a game varies depending on the form of scoring. At duplicate bridge, a 50% game should generally be bid. At IMPs, a 37% game should be bid when vulnerable; a 45% game should be bid when not vulnerable. At rubber bridge and Chicago, slightly more than 50% games should be bid when not vulnerable; slightly less than 50% games should be bid when vulnerable.

VALUES (VALUATION)
Determining the strengths and weaknesses of a hand. One of the most difficult aspects of the modern competitive game is accurately judging the value of a hand.

VALUE SWISS RAISES
As used in the Aces Scientific System, this convention permits the responder to show trump support suitable for a force to game, to deny a singleton or a good five-card suit, and to specify the high card strength on which his raise is based.

VANDERBILT CLUB SYSTEM
The original one club forcing system, developed by Harold S. Vanderbilt, the inventor of Contract Bridge.

VANDERBILT TROPHY
See WORLD CHAMPIONSHIPS.

VARIABLE NO TRUMP

An opening 1NT bid being weak when not vulnerable and strong when vulnerable.

VENICE CUP

See WORLD CHAMPIONSHIPS.

VERIFY

Agreeing to the score. In a pairs game, an East-West player initials the pick-up slip. In a Swiss Teams, the losing team turns its ticket over to the winning team to be brought to the scoring area.

BARON BARCLAY BRIDGE SUPPLIES						Form 6235

N—S PAIR	ALL DEALS PLAYED THIS ROUND WILL BE SCORED ON THIS CARD. CIRCLE DIRECTION OF DECLARER.			E—W OK RSB		E—W PAIR
1						1

N—S SCORE	MADE	DOWN	N—S CONTRACT	BOARD NUMBER	E—W CONTRACT	MADE	DOWN	E—W SCORE
				1	2H	2		110
50				2	4S			

USE BOTTOM HALF FIRST — TEAR AT PERFORATION

VICTORY POINTS

In team events the I.M.P difference in each match is sometimes converted to victory points according to a pre-determined scale. See INTERNATIONAL MATCH POINTS.

VIENNA COUP
Unblocking play required when a menace is blocked and entries are lacking. A winning card in an opponent's suit is temporarily established, only for it to be lost in a squeeze. The play was first described by James Clay of London, a leading whist authority in the last century. He ascribed its discovery to the best whist player in Vienna, hence its name.

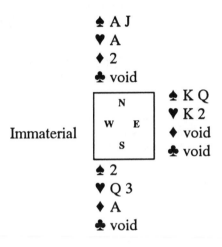

♠ A J
♥ A
♦ 2
♣ void

♠ K Q
♥ K 2
♦ void
♣ void

Immaterial

♠ 2
♥ Q 3
♦ A
♣ void

In this end position, the heart menace is blocked, thus North's heart Ace must be cashed before the diamond is led to squeeze East. See SQUEEZE.

VIENNA SYSTEM
The brainchild of Dr. Paul Stern in 1935, this system features an artificial one club opening bid for hands of relatively normal values and an artificial one notrump opener for strong hands. This is also known as the Austrian System.

VIEW, TO TAKE A
To make a decision concerning the play or a bid.

VINJE SIGNALS
Helge Vinje invented this system which very narrowly defines many distributional patterns on defense. The length of a suit can be shown when leading, following suit or discarding. For example, Vinje's trump signal shows your entire hand pattern by the manner in which the trump suit is followed to. A high-low signal in the trump suit shows one even-numbered suit in your hand and three odd-numbered suits; low-high in the trump suit shows one odd-numbered suit in your hand and three even-numbered suits.

VIOLATION OF PROPRIETIES
When a player disregards a bridge law of conduct. It's usually through accident or ignorance.

VIOLATION OF SYSTEM
When a player knowingly deviates from a partnership bidding agreement for tactical purposes.

VOID
A holding of no cards in a suit.

VOID SHOWING BIDS
The use of an unusual jump to show a void in a side suit has found a place in many of the modern systems. In some methods no distinction is made initially between voids and singletons. It is possible to show a void in responding to a Blackwood inquiry of 4NT by making the normal response one level higher than usual, for example, a 6♣ response showing one Ace and a working void. Another method involves specifying which void is held, by jumping to the suit below the trump suit with a low-ranking void and six of the trump suit with a high-ranking void. See CUE BID, SPLINTER BID.

VROOM
A system of two-suited overcalls for defensive bidding against a strong notrump opening. The system also allows the overcaller to show one-suited hands containing a long major suit.

VU-GRAPH
Method of showing a significant match to a large audience. This is used frequently in national and world championships. See BRIDGE-O-RAMA.

VULNERABILITY
Condition in the scoring, achieved when one game has been won towards completion of the rubber.

VULNERABLE
Term used to describe a side with a game. See NON-VULNER-ABLE, RED, WHITE.

WAITING BID
A non-committal bid, often a cheap forcing bid offering partner more time to describe his hand.

WAIVE A PENALTY
To allow an opponent's transgression of the bridge rules to go unpunished.

WALLET
Device used to hold cards while they are being moved in a duplicate event. See POCKET for photo.

WALSH SYSTEM
Popularly known as West Coast Scientific, this system, formulated principally by Richard Walsh, features: 5 card majors, forcing NT response, strong NT's, non-forcing Stayman, Jacoby Transfer Bids, inverted minor suit raises, two over one game force, and responsive and negative doubles.

W.B.F.
See WORLD BRIDGE FEDERATION.

WEAK FOUR BIDS
An opening bid at the four level made with preemptive intent. See PREEMPTIVE BID, RULE OF TWO AND THREE.

WEAK JUMP OVERCALL
A jump overcall based on a six card suit and about 6-10 points.

WEAK JUMP SHIFT RESPONSES
The use of a jump shift in response to an opening bid of one of a suit to show a weak hand.

WEAK NO TRUMP
An opening bid of 1NT, usually showing 12-14 points and a balanced hand.

WEAK TAKE OUT (WEAKNESS TAKE OUT)
A natural response, especially to an opening 1NT, which does not promise any strength, but merely expresses the wish to play in an alternative denomination. See TAKEOUT.

WEAK THREE BIDS
An opening bid at the three level made with preemptive intent. See PREEMPTIVE BID, RULE OF TWO AND THREE.

WEAK TWO BIDS
An opening bid at the two level with mainly preemptive intent, typically with 6-10 points and a six card suit. A 2NT response is usually an inquiry asking about the strength and suit quality.

WEISSBERGER
A convention played in conjunction with Stayman, designed to locate three card majors in opener's hand.

WEISS CONVENTION
Used over preempts, a double is optional (balanced strength and penalty oriented) and the bid of the cheaper minor suit is used for takeout.

WEST
One of the positions at the bridge table.

WESTERN CUE BID
See CALIFORNIA CUE BID.

WHIST

The forerunner of modern bridge. Whist is a trick-taking game with trumps and partnerships, but no dummy. The card playing techniques of the two games are essentially the same, so as Whist gave way to bridge in the 1930's, many of the top Whist players quickly became the leading bridge players. Some of the movements in use at bridge tournaments today were originally developed for Whist tournaments.

WHITE

Shorthand for describing the situation when neither side is vulnerable. See NON-VULNERABLE, RED, VULNERABLE.

WIDE OPEN

A player is said to have a suit "wide open" if he has no guard in that suit in a no trump contract, or no control in that suit in a slam contract.

WINKLE SQUEEZE

Named and analyzed by Terence Reese. The name is just a memory aid, the position actually being a blocked exit squeeze. In the position shown, declarer needs three of the last four tricks.

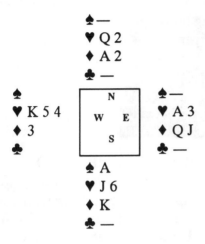

```
              ♠ —
              ♥ Q 2
              ♦ A 2
              ♣ —
  ♠                        ♠ —
  ♥ K 5 4    ┌─────────┐   ♥ A 3
  ♦ 3        │ N       │   ♦ Q J
  ♣         │ W   E   │   ♣ —
            │    S    │
            └─────────┘
              ♠ A
              ♥ J 6
              ♦ K
              ♣ —
```

When the ace of spades is cashed, East-West are caught (dummy discards the two of hearts). East cannot throw a diamond (South would then overtake the king of diamonds with the ace and the two would be a winner), so he must discard a heart. If the three of hearts is thrown, South cashes the king of diamonds and exits with the six of hearts. East is in and must give dummy the last trick with the ace of diamonds. If East tries the spectacular play of unblocking the ace of hearts on the ace of spades, then West is forced to win (or let dummy's queen win) and must then give South the last trick with the jack of hearts.

WINNER

    1) The card that wins the trick.

    2) The highest-ranking card or any card that has been promoted to such a rank through the earlier play.

    3) The person, pair or team that finishes first in an event.

WITHDRAWING A CARD

Permitted only in correcting a revoke before it becomes established or by an opponent following the correction of a revoke, or following a revoke on the twelfth trick.

Bobby Wolff

WOLFF SIGNOFF OVER 2 NOTRUMP REBID

When the opener makes a jump rebid of two notrump after a responder's one-over-one response, the responder with a weak hand may want to play in no more than three of a suit. The Wolff Convention is a three-club bid by responder over the opener's jump to two notrump. This bid asks the opener to bid three of the responder's suit if he has three-card support, a call which the responder can pass.

WONDER BIDS

A conventional system of bids used against a strong club system. They are usually played when vulnerable, while IDAK (Instant Destroyer and Killer) bids are usually played when non-vulnerable.

WOODSON TWO WAY NOTRUMP

A system featuring an opening bid of one notrump to show either 10-12 or 16-18 HCP.

WORKING CARD

A card is said to be working if it is particularly useful, such as a King or Queen in a suit bid by partner.

WORLD BRIDGE FEDERATION (W.B.F.)
The governing authority of international bridge.

WORLD CHAMPIONSHIPS
There are several World Championships:

TEAMS OLYMPIAD
This is contested every four years. Entry is open to every country (affiliated to the W.B.F.) who may enter one team in each category, the open and the ladies. The winners of the open category receive the Vanderbilt Trophy.

BERMUDA BOWL
This is contested every two years. Entry is open to the open champions of every W.B.F. zone (approximately every continent). In recent years the bigger zones have been allowed to enter more than one team.

VENICE CUP
This is contested every two years. Entry is open to the ladies champions of every W.B.F. zone (approximately every continent). In recent years the bigger zones have been allowed to enter more than one team.

PAIRS OLYMPIAD
This is contested every four years. Entry is open to every country (affiliated to the W.B.F.) who may enter several pairs in each category, the number depending on the size of the country. There are three categories - open, ladies and mixed. The winners of the open receive the Schwab Trophy (which was originally presented to the winners of a challenge match played in 1933 between Great Britain and the U.S.A.). In recent years a teams championship has been conducted in parallel with the pairs events, the winners receiving the Rosenblum Trophy. In 1990 the event was retitled a World Championship and three other world titles were introduced - junior, senior and continuous pairs, the last being open to anyone eliminated from the other championships.

WORTHLESS SINGLETON/DOUBLETON
One (singleton) or two (doubleton) small cards in a suit.

WRIGGLE
A convention whereby after an opening 1NT bid has been doubled, the responder with a weak hand attempts to locate a fit which will hopefully prove less costly than standing the double. A redouble shows clubs and another suit. A bid of 2♣ shows either clubs or a two-suited hand without clubs. Other responses are natural weakness take out bids.

WRITTEN BIDDING
The use of a paper pad to record bids. Instead of making their bids vocally, players write them on a pad which is passed to each other. See SCREEN.

WRONG SIDE
A hand is said to be played from the wrong side when the declarer is disadvantaged by the opening lead. If partner were the declarer, either that suit would not have been led or it would not have been so disadvantageous.

𝔛 𝔜 𝔃

X

1) Symbol used in recording hands when the x denotes a small card.

2) Symbol used when writing down a contract to denote that it is doubled (for example, 4Hx). Similarly, two symbols denote that it is doubled and redoubled (for example 4Hxx).

YARBOROUGH

A hand containing no card higher than a nine, named after the English Lord who offered odds of a 1000 to 1 against holding such a hand (the true odds are 1827 to 1).

ZERO

Lowest score possible on a board at duplicate. See BOTTOM.

ZIP SWISS

A fast-paced team competition, comprised of five matches of five boards each with a time allotment of five minutes per board. Most frequently played after the regular sessions of the day have been completed; i.e., Midnight Zip Swiss. See SPEEDBALL.

OFFICIAL (Mitchell or Howell) TRAVELING SCORE

Bid, play and score this board without comment and proceed immediately to the next.
NORTH PLAYER only keeps score

ENTER PAIR NO. OF E-W PAIR   Board No. ___9___

N-S Pair	E-W Pair	CON-TRACT	BY	MADE	DOWN	FINAL SCORE North South	FINAL SCORE East West	E-W Match Points	N-S Match Points
1	6	4S	N	4		420			2
2	1	7S	N		3		150		0
3	3	3NT	S	4		430			3
4	5	4S	N	6		480			5
5	7	6S	N	6		980			6
6	2	4S	N	5		450			4
7	4	6S	N		1		50		1
8								1	6
9								2	2
10								3	3
11								4	5
12								5	1
13								6	4
14								7	0

Indulge in post-mortems, if you must, only at end of round. Play congenially. Announce or display private conventions. Refrain from giving lessons, especially to opponents. Do not make your own rulings; call your game director, that's his job. Count your cards before and after.

BARON BARCLAY BRIDGE SUPPLIES   #7274
1-800-274-2221

Bibliography

ACBL, *The Official Encyclopedia of Bridge*, 4th Edition (1984, Crown)

The Bridge Player's Dictionary (1991, Mr. Bridge Ltd.)

Coffin, *Endplays in Bridge* (1981, Dover)

Culbertson, *The Encyclopedia of Bridge* (1935, *The Bridge World*)

de Satnick, *Everyone's Introduction to Bridge Conventions* (1984, Avon)

Easy Guide to Duplicate Bridge (1984, ACBL)

Jacoby-Morehead, *The Fireside Book of Cards* (1957, Simon & Schuster)

Kearse, *Bridge Conventions Complete* (1990, Devyn)

McMullin, *Adventures in Duplicate Bridge* (1988, ACBL)

Penick, *Beginning Bridge Complete* (1985, Devyn)

Root-Pavlicek, *Modern Bridge Conventions* (1981, Crown)

Reese, *Bridge Conventions, Finesses and Coups* (1965, Sterling)

Reese, *Bridge Player's Dictionary* (1959, Sterling)

Stewart-Baron, *The Bridge Book, Volume 1* (1988, Devyn)

I hope this first edition of The *Bridge Player's Dictionary* is a valuable reference guide for you. I plan to update it when the next edition is published. Any new entries, corrections, suggestions or comments you have will be greatly appreciated. Please write to me at our address below.

Thank you,

Randall Baron, Editor

DEVYN PRESS, INC.
3600 Chamberlain Lane, Suite 230
Louisville, KY 40241

RANDALL BARON has been producing and editing bridge publications since he founded Baron Bridge Supplies in 1974. A well-known teacher and expert, he has become America's leading bridge publisher as president of Devyn Press. He is also the author of over 20 acclaimed books on bridge, baseball, basketball and horse racing. A graduate of the University of Florida, he resides in his native Louisville, Kentucky, with his wife Mary, their teenagers Devyn and Dustin, and their faithful cocker spaniel, Vickie.

DEVYN PRESS, INC.

3600 Chamberlain Lane, Suite 230, Louisville, KY 40241

Andersen THE LEBENSOHL CONVENTION COMPLETE	$ 6.95
Baron THE BRIDGE PLAYER'S DICTIONARY	$19.95
Bergen BETTER BIDDING WITH BERGEN, Vol. I, Uncontested Auctions	$ 9.95
Bergen BETTER BIDDING WITH BERGEN, Vol. II, Competitive Auctions	$ 9.95
Blackwood COMPLETE BOOK OF OPENING LEADS	$12.95
Blackwood & Hanson PLAY FUNDAMENTALS	$ 6.95
Bruno-Hardy 2 OVER 1 GAME FORCE: AN INTRODUCTION	$ 9.95
Cole FISHHEADS	$ 7.95
DeSerpa THE MEXICAN CONTRACT	$ 5.95
Eber & Freeman HAVE I GOT A STORY FOR YOU	$ 7.95
Feldheim FIVE CARD MAJOR BIDDING IN CONTRACT BRIDGE	$ 9.95
Flannery THE FLANNERY 2 DIAMOND OPENING	$ 7.95
Goldman ACES SCIENTIFIC	$ 9.95
Goldman WINNERS AND LOSERS AT THE BRIDGE TABLE	$ 3.95
Goodwin LET'S PLAY CARDS	$ 9.95
Groner DUPLICATE BRIDGE DIRECTION	$11.95
Hardy SPLINTERS AND OTHER SHORTNESS BIDS	$ 7.95
Hardy TWO-OVER-ONE GAME FORCE	$12.95
Harris BRIDGE DIRECTOR'S COMPANION (2nd Edition)	$14.95
Karpin THE DRAWING OF TRUMPS — AND ITS POSTPONEMENT	$ 9.95
Karpin PLAY OF THE CARDS QUIZ BOOK	$ 9.95
Kearse BRIDGE CONVENTIONS COMPLETE, 1990 Edition	$24.95
Kelsey	
COUNTDOWN TO BETTER BRIDGE	$ 9.95
Lampert THE FUN WAY TO ADVANCED BRIDGE	$ 8.95
Lawrence	
CARD COMBINATIONS	$11.95
COMPLETE BOOK ON BALANCING	$11.95
COMPLETE BOOK ON OVERCALLS	$ 9.95
DYNAMIC DEFENSE	$11.95
FALSECARDS	$ 9.95
HAND EVALUATION	$11.95
HOW TO READ YOUR OPPONENTS' CARDS	$ 9.95
JUDGMENT AT BRIDGE	$ 9.95
PARTNERSHIP UNDERSTANDINGS	$ 3.95
PLAY BRIDGE WITH MIKE LAWRENCE	$ 9.95
PLAY SWISS TEAMS WITH MIKE LAWRENCE	$ 7.95
WORKBOOK ON THE TWO OVER ONE SYSTEM	$11.95
Lawrence & Hanson WINNING BRIDGE INTANGIBLES	$ 4.95
Lipkin INVITATION TO ANNIHILATION	$ 8.95
Machlin TOURNAMENT BRIDGE: AN UNCENSORED MEMOIR	$ 5.95
Michaels & Cohen 4-3-2-1 MANUAL	$ 2.95
Penick BEGINNING BRIDGE COMPLETE	$ 6.95
Penick BEGINNING BRIDGE QUIZZES	$ 6.95
Powell TICKETS TO THE DEVIL	$ 5.95
Reese PLAY THESE HANDS WITH ME	$ 7.95
Reese & Hoffman PLAY IT AGAIN, SAM	$ 7.95
Rosenkranz	
BRIDGE: THE BIDDER'S GAME	$12.95
TIPS FOR TOPS	$ 9.95
TRUMP LEADS	$ 7.95
MORE TIPS FOR TOPS	$ 9.95
Rosenkranz & Alder BID TO WIN, PLAY FOR PLEASURE	$11.95
Rosenkranz & Truscott: BIDDING ON TARGET	$10.95
Rubens & Lukacs TEST YOUR PLAY AS DECLARER, Vol. 1	$ 5.95
Silverman	
ELEMENTARY BRIDGE FIVE CARD MAJOR STUDENT TEXT	$ 2.75
INTERMEDIATE BRIDGE FIVE CARD MAJOR STUDENT TEXT	$ 2.95
ADVANCED & DUPLICATE BRIDGE STUDENT TEXT	$ 2.95
PLAY OF THE HAND AS DECLARER & DEFENDER STUDENT TEXT	$ 2.95
Sontag & Steinberg IMPROVE YOUR BRIDGE — FAST	$ 4.95
Stern EXPERT BRIDGE	$ 6.95
Stewart & Baron	
THE BRIDGE BOOK, Vol. 1, Beginning	$ 9.95
THE BRIDGE BOOK, Vol. 2, Intermediate	$ 9.95
THE BRIDGE BOOK, Vol. 3, Advanced	$ 7.95
THE BRIDGE BOOK, Vol. 4, Defense	$ 7.95
Von Elsner	
THE ACE OF SPIES	$ 5.95
CRUISE BRIDGE	$ 5.95
EVERYTHING'S JAKE WITH ME	$ 5.95
THE BEST OF JAKE WINKMAN	$ 5.95
THE JAKE OF HEARTS	$ 5.95
THE JAKE OF DIAMONDS	$ 5.95
Woolsey	
MATCHPOINTS	$11.95
MODERN DEFENSIVE SIGNALLING	$ 4.95
PARTNERSHIP DEFENSE	$ 9.95

CALL TOLL FREE IN THE U.S. & CANADA
1-800-274-2221
TO ORDER OR TO REQUEST OUR 64 PAGE FULL COLOR
CATALOG OF BRIDGE BOOKS, SUPPLIES AND GIFTS.